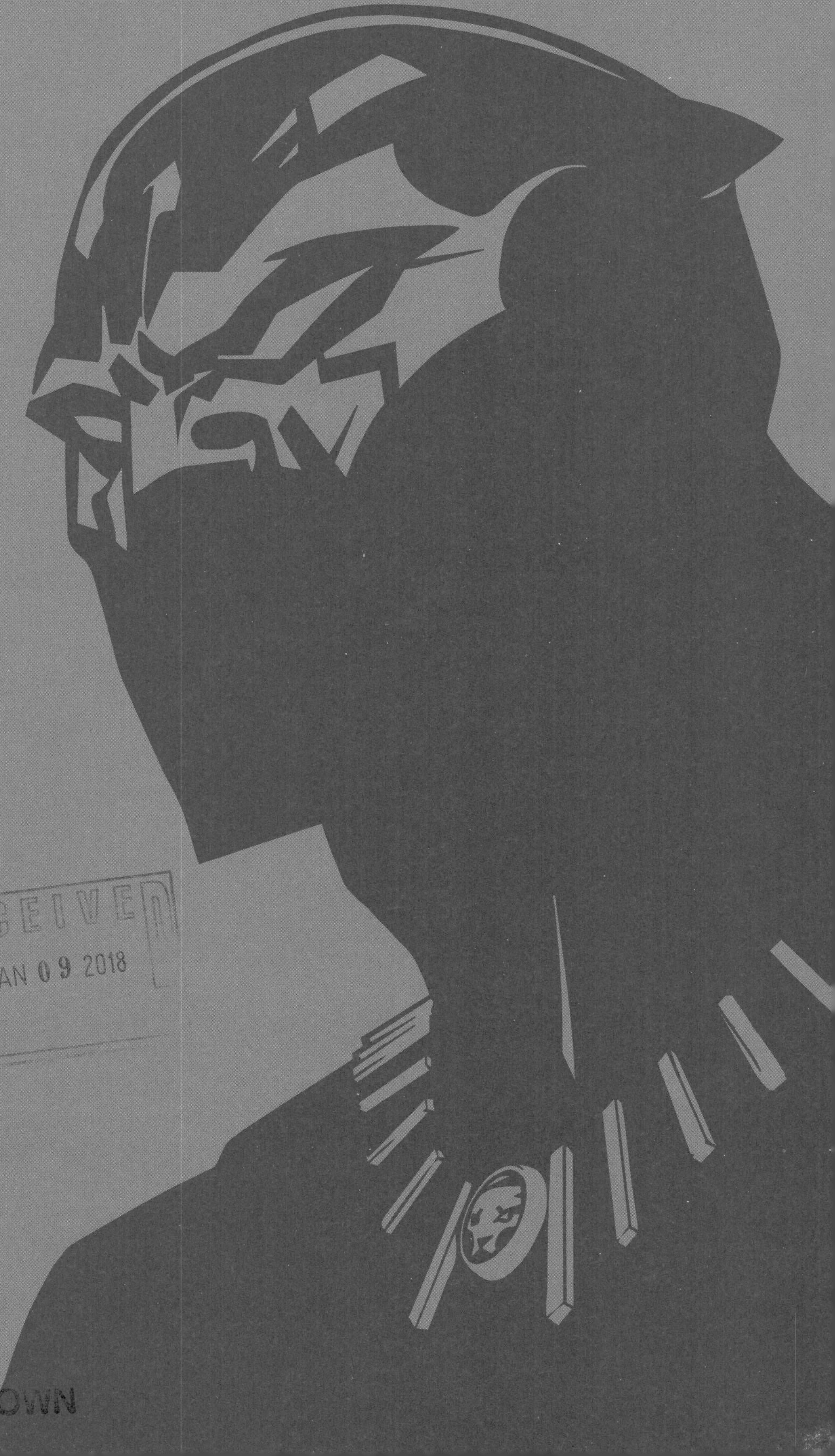

MARVEL

BLACK PANTHER

Senior Editor Cefn Ridout
Senior Designer Anne Sharples
Picture Researcher Alex Evangeli
Pre-Production Producer Jennifer Murray
Senior Producer Zara Markland
Managing Editor Sadie Smith
Managing Art Editor Vicky Short
Publisher Julie Ferris
Art Director Lisa Lanzarini
Publishing Director Simon Beecroft

Edited for DK by Kathryn Hill
Designed for DK by Dynamo

Cover based on artwork and designs by
Brian Stelfreeze and Manny Mederos

Dorling Kindersley would like to thank:
Brian Overton, Caitlin O'Connell, Jeff Youngquist, and Joe Hochstein at Marvel for
vital help and advice; Jon Hall, Lisa Sodeau, and Abi Wright for design assistance;
Alastair Dougall and Ruth Amos for editorial assistance;
Melanie Scott for proofreading; and Vanessa Bird for the index.

First American Edition, 2018
Published in the United States by DK Publishing
345 Hudson Street, New York, New York 10014

18 19 20 21 22   10 9 8 7 6 5 4 3 2 1
001–305700–Jan/2018

© 2018 MARVEL

Published in Great Britain by Dorling Kindersley Limited.
A catalog record for this book is available from the Library of Congress.
ISBN: 978-1-4654-6626-6

DK books are available at special discounts when purchased in bulk
for sales promotions, premiums, fundraising, or educational use.
For details, contact: DK Publishing Special Markets, 345 Hudson Street,
New York, New York 10014 SpecialSales@dk.com

Printed and bound in China

A WORLD OF IDEAS:
SEE ALL THERE IS TO KNOW
www.dk.com

MARVEL

BLACK PANTHER

THE ULTIMATE GUIDE

WRITTEN BY
STEPHEN "WIN" WIACEK

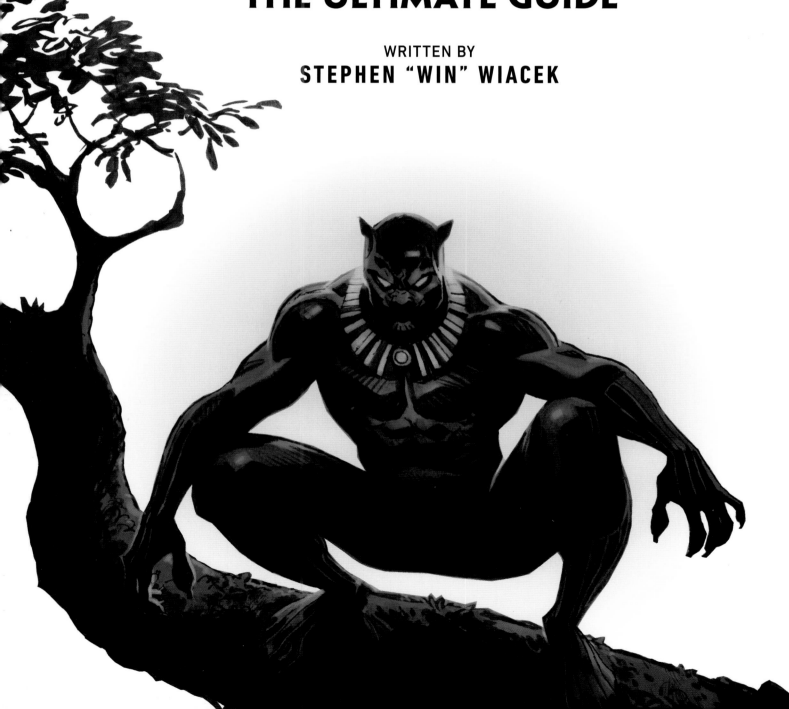

CONTENTS

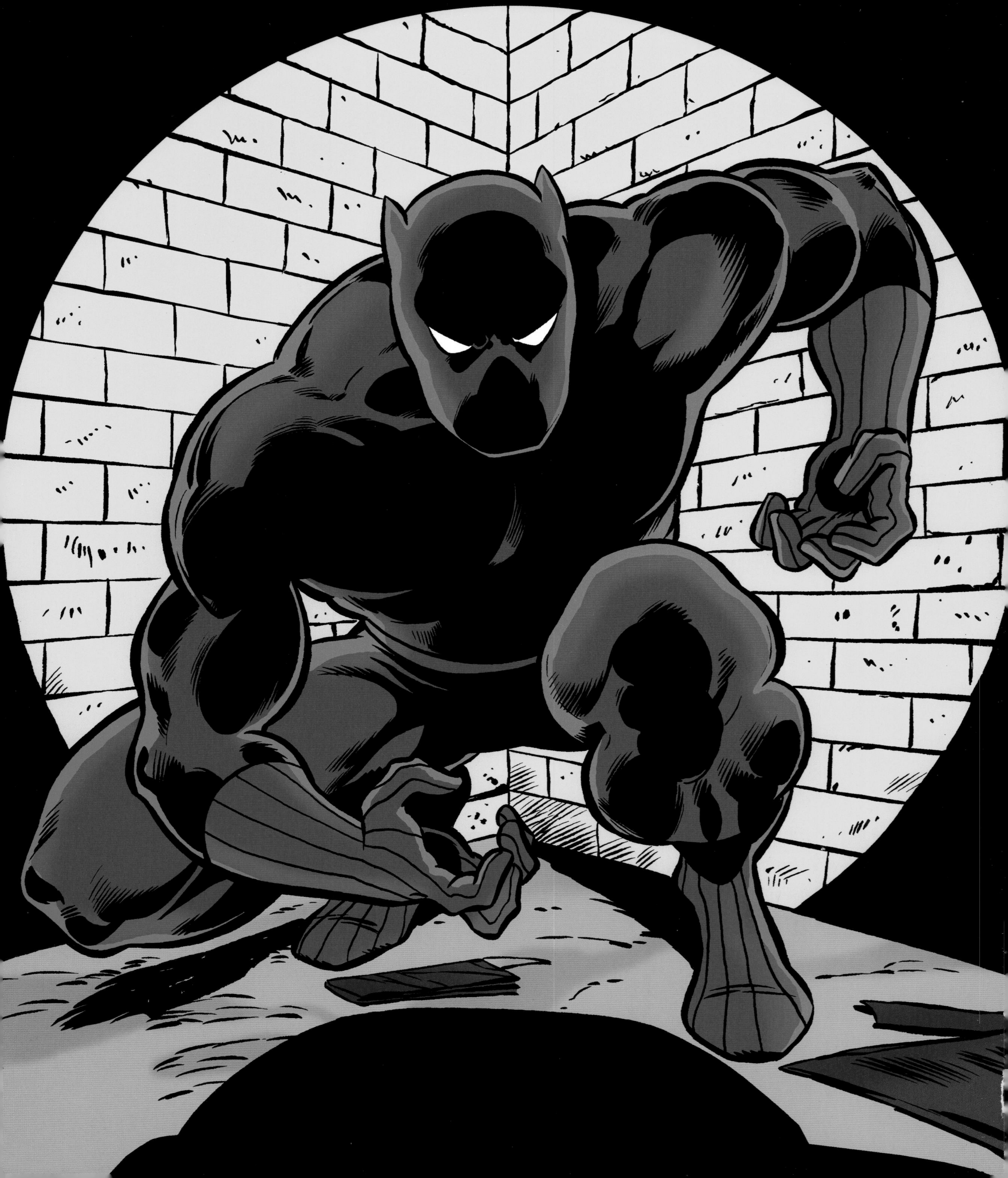

It is impossible to adequately cover the half-century trail of the Black Panther in this foreword. And I should know. I spent nearly five years trying to hear T'Challa's voice in my head; to know him as intimately as anyone in my real life.

In the 1960s, when the Black Panther first leapt at the unsuspecting reader, there had never been an African Super Hero like him. Pop culture and comics were spectacularly altered when Jack Kirby and Stan Lee gave birth to this king of the hidden, technologically advanced nation of Wakanda. The Panther wasn't merely the first black Super Hero to invade the almost exclusively white world of the genre, but he was also the only African comics hero who didn't conform to the streetwise Blaxploitation cliché that dominated 1970s pop culture.

When the Panther debuted over two memorable issues of the *Fantastic Four*, there was scant space to explore Wakanda or the regions beyond the Royal Palace. And, as the '70s progressed, some of T'Challa's uniqueness would be lost when he was brought to the U.S. to join the Avengers and become part of Manhattan's coterie of costumed heroes.

Marvel returned the king to his kingdom in *Jungle Action.* That's when I came to think seriously about T'Challa and his world as I had been assigned the series, which was seen as having little commercial potential. If Tarzan comics were a hard sell, what chance did an African king stand? However, Wakanda was an amazing secret world that T'Challa kept diligently hidden. It was a high-tech wonderland, filled with riches gained from its huge cache of rare Vibranium ore. It also boasted a diverse culture of farmers, technocrats, religious leaders, and more.

I always saw T'Challa as a leader who tried to represent all his people. He was a king who cared and understood what each individual culture brought to Wakanda to make the country self-sufficient. So it didn't take me long to realize that all the characters would be Wakandan or African. It wasn't an easy stand to take. But I was fortunate that artist Rich Buckler and I had become friends, and Rich had the clout to make it happen. We worked day and night to make the Panther and his world a reality. I would sometimes pose in Panther-ish crouches that I felt captured the poetry of T'Challa's movement.

I also knew this new series needed a compelling villain who would appear over several issues. Otherwise Wakandans might think it would be more peaceful without T'Challa around, if his return always seemed to attract a succession of super-powered bad guys determined to threaten their way of life. This led to the creation of Killmonger, who wanted to usurp T'Challa's throne by any means necessary. I titled the story "Panther's Rage" and began mapping out the immediate terrain as well as the next series, "Panther's Quest," which would take T'Challa to apartheid South Africa in search of his missing stepmother. I felt that such a human theme would also allow me to examine a racist regime.

However, circumstances made me decide against that storyline in 1976, and it wasn't until the 1980s that I finally had the chance to work with editor Terry Kavanagh and artist Gene Colan (who I loved dearly) on "Panther's Quest." When Gene wasn't available for the next story, "Panther's Prey," which returned T'Challa to Wakanda, I made one of my best art decisions, choosing Dwayne Turner to mark the occasion.

Indeed, I had such glorious partners and friends on these books—Rich Buckler, Billy Graham, Gene Colan, and Dwayne Turner. In later years, the "Great Cat's" trail set off in different directions, as talented writers and artists like Christopher Priest, Reginald Hudlin, Peter B. Gillis, Denys Cowan, and Dwayne MacDuffie brought their personal visions to T'Challa's exploits.

When I started writing Black Panther, I couldn't imagine the kind of promotion for Ta-Nehisi Coates and Brian Stelfreeze's latest chronicle in T'Challa's life. But I don't have to imagine how great it is to see the global media spotlight on the King of Wakanda.

Enjoy following the Black Panther's long and distinctive trail in this book. I know I will. Just as I know I will hear a vestige of T'Challa's voice in my head for the rest of my days.

DON MCGREGOR
RHODE ISLAND, JUNE 12, 2017

THE 1960S WAS A TIME OF GREAT CHANGE. The U.S. was experiencing a social, cultural, and political revolution as a new generation questioned old values and entrenched traditions, especially on the divisive issue of racial equality.

Introduced in the summer of 1966, the Black Panther was a genuinely radical concept and character, even by the standards of Marvel Comics. The fledgling U.S. comics publisher had fast established a reputation for challenging the status quo. And the Panther perfectly caught the mood of the times.

Here was a black Super Hero who faced the world on his own uncompromising terms. And as an African king ruling a country more culturally and technologically progressive than the U.S., the Black Panther easily matched his fellow costumed crusaders in power, competency, complexity, and resources. His success also paved the way for other black Marvel Super Heroes like the Falcon, Luke Cage, Black Goliath, and Blade.

Yet most exciting for readers of the Panther's fantastic adventures was the regular sight of a black role model winning against the odds for the benefit of everyone.

Black Panther has always been blessed with authors and artists of singular vision. Creators Stan Lee and Jack Kirby imagined a powerful champion who could master any situation, while successor Roy Thomas used the hero's tenure with the Avengers to confront social issues making headlines across the U.S.

Philosophical scribe Don McGregor, alongside artistic collaborators Rich Buckler, Billy Graham, and Gene Colan, redefined the character for the modern era, breaking new ground when T'Challa finally landed his own series in 1973. Their epic run of politically charged tales took place in a fully realized fictional African kingdom, Wakanda, and featured an all-black cast of heroes, villains, and supporting players.

Later, under Christopher Priest, the Panther became scary and satirical, while successive writers such as Reginald Hudlin, David Liss, and, more recently, acclaimed journalist Ta-Nehisi Coates, have reshaped T'Challa to suit changing times. These wordsmiths and the artists with whom they worked have made Black Panther relevant and trailblazing time and again.

Fifty years after his comic book debut, the Black Panther made a dramatic entrance on the big screen in *Captain America: Civil War*. In 2018, he takes center stage in his own film. It cements his place in the Marvel Universe as an enduring beacon of hope and the very epitome of a cool and capable modern hero.

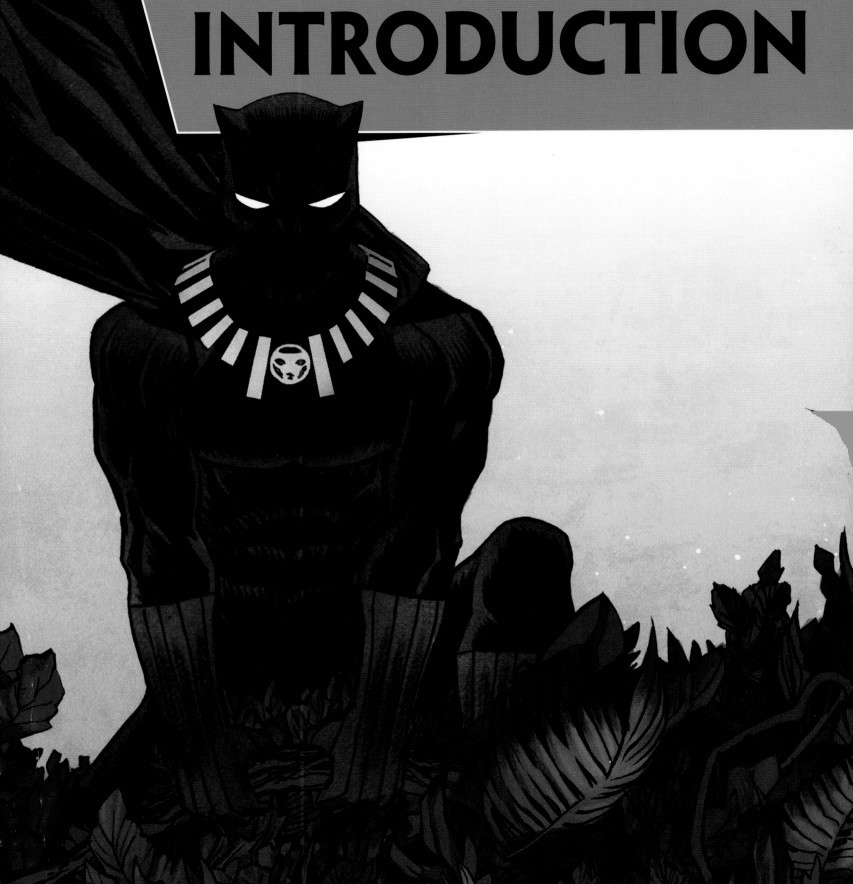

INTRODUCTION

MAN OF THE MOMENT

*"I shall be as **strong**...and as **fearless** as the sacred **Black Panther!**"* T'CHALLA

The 1960s saw U.S. popular culture confront decades of racial discrimination. In a medium where black people were still depicted as primitive natives or servants, if seen at all, Marvel Comics was at the forefront of a new movement. African-American supporting characters began showing up in many of its comics, such as Gabe Jones in *Sgt. Fury and His Howling Commandos* and Joseph "Robbie" Robertson in *The Amazing Spider-Man*. These men were remarkable enough, but in 1966, Stan Lee and Jack Kirby took the next logical, if controversial and commercially risky, step. They created the first black Super Hero to appear in America—in one of Marvel Comics' best-selling titles at the time, *Fantastic Four*.

As the character developed, the Black Panther evolved from a singular and resourceful lone warrior into the latest and greatest example of a dynasty of heroic champions stretching back into prehistory. Over the decades, his sleek, dark costume has remained remarkably unchanged, with necessary modifications and enhancements to suit the times.

MARVEL COMICS GROUP

Fan Four

Introducing: THE SENSATIONAL BLACK PANTHER!

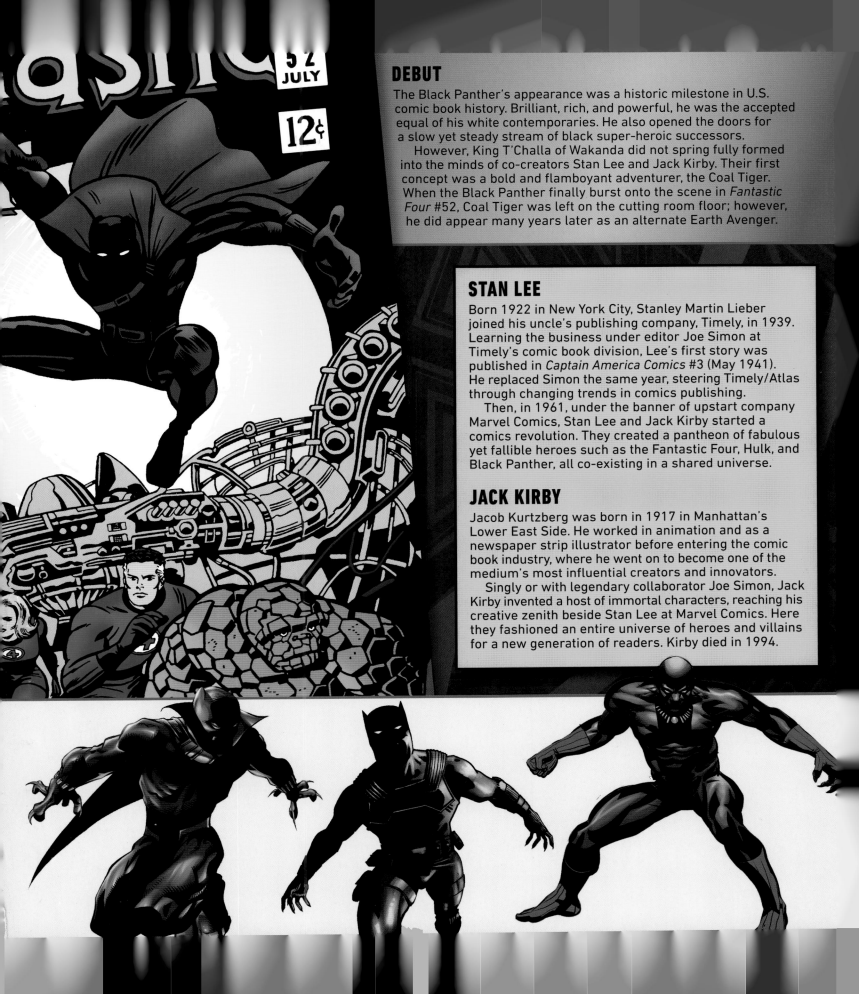

52 JULY

12¢

DEBUT

The Black Panther's appearance was a historic milestone in U.S. comic book history. Brilliant, rich, and powerful, he was the accepted equal of his white contemporaries. He also opened the doors for a slow yet steady stream of black super-heroic successors.

However, King T'Challa of Wakanda did not spring fully formed into the minds of co-creators Stan Lee and Jack Kirby. Their first concept was a bold and flamboyant adventurer, the Coal Tiger. When the Black Panther finally burst onto the scene in *Fantastic Four* #52, Coal Tiger was left on the cutting room floor; however, he did appear many years later as an alternate Earth Avenger.

STAN LEE

Born 1922 in New York City, Stanley Martin Lieber joined his uncle's publishing company, Timely, in 1939. Learning the business under editor Joe Simon at Timely's comic book division, Lee's first story was published in *Captain America Comics* #3 (May 1941). He replaced Simon the same year, steering Timely/Atlas through changing trends in comics publishing.

Then, in 1961, under the banner of upstart company Marvel Comics, Stan Lee and Jack Kirby started a comics revolution. They created a pantheon of fabulous yet fallible heroes such as the Fantastic Four, Hulk, and Black Panther, all co-existing in a shared universe.

JACK KIRBY

Jacob Kurtzberg was born in 1917 in Manhattan's Lower East Side. He worked in animation and as a newspaper strip illustrator before entering the comic book industry, where he went on to become one of the medium's most influential creators and innovators.

Singly or with legendary collaborator Joe Simon, Jack Kirby invented a host of immortal characters, reaching his creative zenith beside Stan Lee at Marvel Comics. Here they fashioned an entire universe of heroes and villains for a new generation of readers. Kirby died in 1994.

START

N'yami dies soon after giving birth to T'Chaka's firstborn son, T'Challa.

Young T'Challa discovers his brother Hunter is torturing citizens as head of the *Hatut Zeraze* secret police.

Sent to study abroad, T'Challa graduates from Oxford University and completes his studies in the U.S. During T'Challa's absence N'Baza rules Wakanda.

T'Challa's best friend B'Tumba is exposed as an A.I.M. agent, stealing Vibranium for the science terrorists.

Black Panther T'Chaka and Queen N'Yami adopt white orphan Hunter to raise as their son.

T'Chaka's second wife Ramonda gives birth to T'Challa's half-sister, Shuri.

Queen Ramonda vanishes and all mention of her is forbidden at court.

Teenaged T'Challa undergoes his walkabout manhood ritual and meets young orphan Ororo.

Klaw invades Wakanda and murders T'Chaka. He is driven off by the returned Prince T'Challa, who becomes known as the "Orphan King."

When Monica Lynne's sister is murdered, T'Challa investigates and is captured and brainwashed by the Dragon Circle Cult.

After a year of conflict, Killmonger dies in the final battle against Black Panther.

Back in Africa, T'Challa searches for King Solomon's Frogs with Abner Little.

T'Challa meets the Falcon and constructs devices enabling him to fly like a bird.

Erik Killmonger tries to conquer Wakanda using super-powered minions and dinosaurs.

Unknown to anyone, King Solomon's Frogs materialize T'Challa's future self in the present.

Black Panther invades Kiber Island to stop a madman consuming the life energy of Wakandans.

Monica Lynne and Kevin Trublood restore T'Challa's suppressed memories and he crushes the Dragon Circle cult.

T'Challa's half-brother Jakarra uses raw Vibranium to mutate himself into a world-shattering monster.

T'Challa opens a Wakandan embassy in New York and is ambushed by Klaw.

War between Wakanda and Atlantis is narrowly averted by the Defenders.

PANTHER TRACKS

The latest in an ancient, unbroken line of heroes, T'Challa guides his people through the most tumultuous periods of Wakanda's history. Here are some of the key moments in Black Panther's remarkable story.

Timeline key

⬤ Cosmic shifts

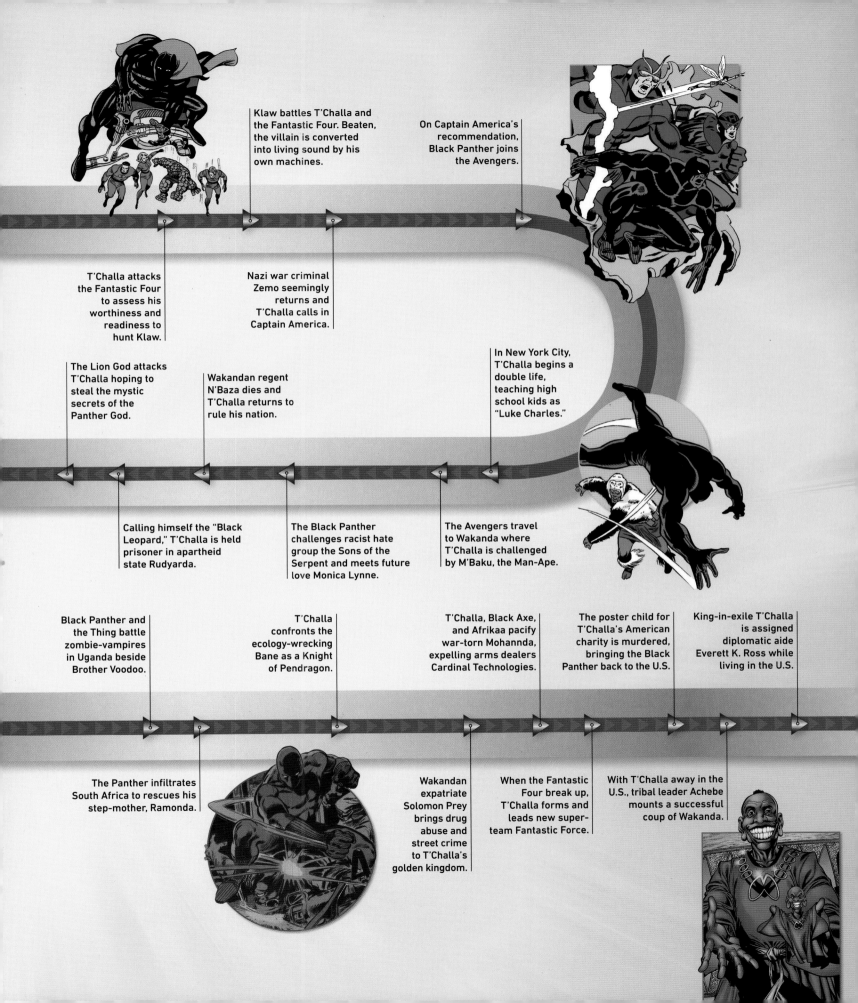

Klaw battles T'Challa and the Fantastic Four. Beaten, the villain is converted into living sound by his own machines.

On Captain America's recommendation, Black Panther joins the Avengers.

T'Challa attacks the Fantastic Four to assess his worthiness and readiness to hunt Klaw.

Nazi war criminal Zemo seemingly returns and T'Challa calls in Captain America.

The Lion God attacks T'Challa hoping to steal the mystic secrets of the Panther God.

Wakandan regent N'Baza dies and T'Challa returns to rule his nation.

In New York City, T'Challa begins a double life, teaching high school kids as "Luke Charles."

Calling himself the "Black Leopard," T'Challa is held prisoner in apartheid state Rudyarda.

The Black Panther challenges racist hate group the Sons of the Serpent and meets future love Monica Lynne.

The Avengers travel to Wakanda where T'Challa is challenged by M'Baku, the Man-Ape.

Black Panther and the Thing battle zombie-vampires in Uganda beside Brother Voodoo.

T'Challa confronts the ecology-wrecking Bane as a Knight of Pendragon.

T'Challa, Black Axe, and Afrikaa pacify war-torn Mohannda, expelling arms dealers Cardinal Technologies.

The poster child for T'Challa's American charity is murdered, bringing the Black Panther back to the U.S.

King-in-exile T'Challa is assigned diplomatic aide Everett K. Ross while living in the U.S.

The Panther infiltrates South Africa to rescues his step-mother, Ramonda.

Wakandan expatriate Solomon Prey brings drug abuse and street crime to T'Challa's golden kingdom.

When the Fantastic Four break up, T'Challa forms and leads new super-team Fantastic Force.

With T'Challa away in the U.S., tribal leader Achebe mounts a successful coup of Wakanda.

TIMELINE

Demon-lord Mephisto reveals he is helping to sponsor the madman Achebe, who ousted Black Panther from power in Wakanda.

T'Challa's economic manoeuvrings create political confusion and lead to the appointment of Everett Ross as the de facto ruler of Wakanda.

Near death, T'Challa visits the Panther God's realm where he battles dream-demon Nightmare.

Following an alien incursion, T'Challa and Storm rekindle their romantic relationship.

With an international crisis brewing, Hunter attacks T'Challa with his mercenary Dogs of War.

Attempting to remove Achebe and a resurrected Killmonger, T'Challa manipulates the U.S. stock market, crashing the global economy.

Defeating T'Challa in ritual combat, Killmonger becomes the new Black Panther.

T'Challa threatens war with Atlantis and Lemuria to protect a child of Deviant leader Ghaur.

T'Challa defends Hell's Kitchen for Daredevil, earning the title "The Most Dangerous Man Alive."

Shuri becomes the new Black Panther when Doctor Doom kills T'Challa. He is later resurrected by Storm.

Ororo and T'Challa join Human Torch and the Thing in a new, multiverse-roaming Fantastic Four.

To end the Doomwar, T'Challa destroys all the processed Vibranium on Earth.

Deprived of his Panther powers, T'Challa battles to save Wakanda from Doctor Doom.

T'Challa and Storm repel an invasion of Wakanda by shape-shifting alien Skrulls.

U.S. suppression of superhumans grows. T'Challa and Storm join Captain America's anti-government faction.

T'Challa returns to Wakanda and is appointed King of the Dead by Panther God Bast.

Wakanda is smashed by a tidal wave created by a Phoenix-possessed Sub-Mariner.

T'Challa convenes a new Illuminati think tank to combat the threat of incursions after capturing Black Swan.

INFINITY

The Panther and his U.S. allies save Wakanda from a hostile financial takeover by the Kingpin.

Avengers and X-Men go to war over the fate of mutant Hope Summers as the Phoenix Force approaches Earth.

King T'Challa's and Queen Ororo's marriage is annulled as the Avengers/X-Men war concludes.

The multiverse fractures, sparking intergalactic chaos. With most Avengers off-world battling the crisis, Thanos' legions invade Earth.

Shuri dies defending Wakanda when Thanos and Namor's Cabal occupy Necropolis.

Disgraced *Dora Milaje* Nakia captures, torments, and tries to seduce T'Challa.

T'Challa's dying future self is abducted and partially healed by genetic maverick Deadly Nightshade.

Present-day T'Challa receives a fatal brain injury while battling a mind-controlled Iron Fist.

An epic and convoluted plan to uncover and punish XCon begins with T'Challa declaring war on Tony Stark.

T'Challa faces growing unrest as the tribes of Wakanda turn on each other.

Beside his dying future self, T'Challa saves America from being conquered by XCon and the White Wolf.

T'Challa weds X-Man Storm in Wakanda as anti-superhuman legislation provokes a civil war between America's Super Heroes.

An American-led coalition covertly attacks Wakanda with superhumans and zombie soldiers.

While recovering in the U.S., T'Challa trains N.Y.P.D. detective Kasper Cole to be a Black Panther.

The royal newlyweds embark on a world tour of non-aligned nations in the wake of the superhuman civil war.

The Black Panther goes on a worldwide quest for a queen before proposing to his childhood sweetheart Ororo Monroe.

Kasper Cole—now White Tiger—joins a clandestine Crew to clean up the streets of New York.

Two Black Panthers and their modern allies are time-shifted to the Old West and battle Loki to save the Gods of Asgard.

After a timeless period on Battleworld, T'Challa returns to rule Wakanda on a reborn Earth.

Black Panther Shuri returns from the Djalia with incredible new powers.

T'Challa and the Crew investigate the death of an activist connected to the secret history of African-American superhumans.

The Black Panther goes in search of Africa's missing Gods, the Orishas.

FINISH

Reality ends and the Marvel Universe dies as Time Runs Out.

Superhuman revolutionaries Tetu and Zenzi lead the People in an effort to overthrow Wakanda's government.

The Ultimates begin fixing universal problems by curing Galactus of his world-consuming hunger.

TIME RUNS OUT

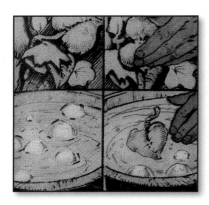

Panther power

As king and protector of Wakanda, and later as an international Super Hero, the Black Panther possesses vastly heightened senses, in addition to enhanced speed, strength, reflexes, durability, healing, and stamina. These augmented attributes come from T'Challa's regular use of a unique heart-shaped herb found in Wakanda. The herb's incredible properties may be magical, Vibranium-mutated, or a combination of both.

ORIGIN

Called Haramu-Fal, the "Orphan King," T'Challa's life is tainted with tragedy. His mother N'Yami dies days after his birth and when his father King T'Chaka remarries, his stepmother Ramonda mysteriously vanishes from court after only a few years. The Prince's responsibilities begin after Wakanda is invaded and T'Chaka is killed by Ulysses Klaw. T'Challa leads the revolt, expelling the occupation forces before being sent abroad to study.

Schooled in Western science and philosophy, T'Challa returns to undergo sacred rites that connect him to the Panther Spirit. Reinforcing Wakanda through his discoveries in the outer world, T'Challa decides to make the Panther known beyond his borders and makes first contact with the famous Fantastic Four.

> *"I am your **king**...that is my **sacred** duty...whenever I fail, whenever Wakandans die, some part of me is lost."*
>
> T'CHALLA

Black cat magic

After dying but being pardoned by the personification of Death, T'Challa revives with a new power set. With his sister Shuri now the Black Panther, T'Challa works with shaman Zawavari, petitioning other gods to restore and magnify his physical abilities. He gains greater resistance to magical attacks and a new "soul sense," allowing him to categorize, identify, and track targets—even Skrulls—by their ethereal auras.

BLACK PANTHER

The Black Panther is the ultimate human predator—a peerless hunter and fighter. T'Challa utilizes supreme intellect, strategic brilliance, physical perfection, and hard-earned combat skills in the service of his beloved Wakanda and the world.

Anti-metal claws for gripping sheer surfaces and supplementing striking power.

The mask is a marvel of cybernetic micro-electronics, activated by mental command.

Vibranium-weave uniform protects against most conventional forms of attack.

DATA FILE

REAL NAME: T'Challa

FIRST APPEARANCE: *Fantastic Four* (Vol. 1) #52 (Jul. 1966)

OCCUPATION: King of Wakanda, Chieftain of Panther Clan, diplomat, scientist, adventurer, former schooleacher

AFFILIATIONS: Panther Cult, Avengers, Fantastic Four, Ultimates, Fantastic Force, Defenders, Secret Avengers, Illuminati, Knights of Pendragon, Wakanda Design Group

POWERS/ABILITIES: Heart-shaped herb-enhanced speed, agility, strength, and reflexes; genius-level intellect; master strategist and tactician

ALIASES: Luke Charles, Black Leopard, Nubian Prince, Coal Tiger, Daredevil

BASE: Wakanda; New York City

King of the Dead

After the multiverse dies and is recreated, T'Challa regains the throne. Repossessing his Panther abilities, he also retains his Soul Sense and gains hyper-cosmic awareness— a precognitive sense of unfolding metaphysical events. This reinforces his position as Wakanda's King of the Dead. He is able to consult with every chieftain to have ruled the nation, commanding their services in the realms beyond.

THE GREAT CAT

T'Challa comes from a line of Warrior Chiefs who have safeguarded Wakanda for millennia. Trained from birth in all aspects of statecraft and martial arts, his education is completed overseas, where he displays amazing accomplishments in all areas of science. Although the blessings of the goddess Bast magnify his physical abilities, T'Challa's greatest weapon is his mind: brilliantly inventive, tactically dazzling, and strategically inspired.

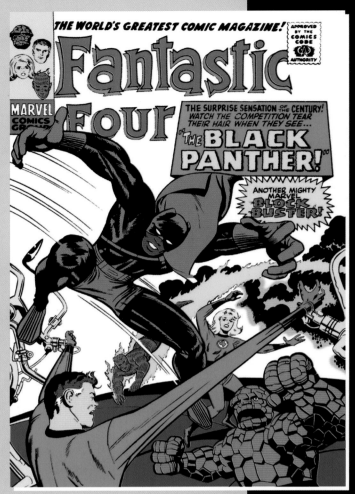

FANTASTIC FOUR (VOL. 1) #52

THE MYSTERIOUS BLACK PANTHER STRIKES! IS HE FRIEND...OR FOE?

The Fantastic Four meet an emissary from an emerging African nation and is drawn into battling an enigmatic and formidable opponent. And so Black Panther makes his debut appearance, testing his prowess against Marvel Comics' first family of heroes.

JULY 1966

MAIN CHARACTERS
T'Challa • Fantastic Four (Reed Richards, Susan Richards, Ben Grimm, Johnny Storm)

SUPPORTING CHARACTERS
Wyatt Wingfoot • T'Challa's emissary

MAIN LOCATIONS
Baxter Building, New York City • Metro College • Techno Organic Jungle, Wakanda

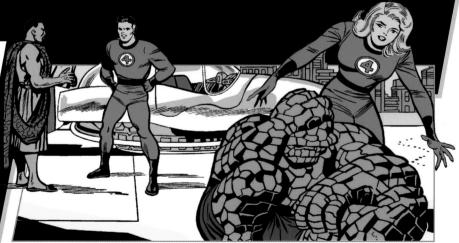

1 After an impressive interview with the representative of a reclusive African monarch known as the Black Panther, Reed Richards wants to find out more about the ruler. Impressed by their visitor's gifts of incredibly advanced technology, the Fantastic Four agree to visit the king in his little-known homeland and join him in "the greatest hunt of all time."

2 In the African nation of Wakanda, the young chieftain named T'Challa greets the news of the Fantastic Four's imminent arrival with great joy. The heroes have no notion that their host intends to stalk them through hostile tropical environments, as well as the artificial electronic jungle he has built beneath Wakanda's primitive-seeming surface settlements.

*"My tale is one of **tragedy**...and deadly **revenge**...!"*

Black Panther

3 Suspecting nothing, the Fantastic Four and the team's Native American friend, Wyatt Wingfoot, arrive in Africa. They are astounded when the verdant jungles give way to a subterranean wonderland of advanced technology. However, before they can catch their collective breath, they are ambushed by a sinister feline figure: the Black Panther.

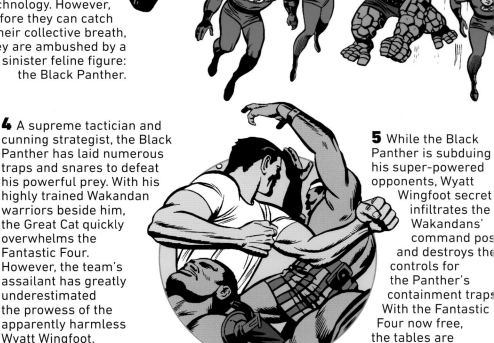

4 A supreme tactician and cunning strategist, the Black Panther has laid numerous traps and snares to defeat his powerful prey. With his highly trained Wakandan warriors beside him, the Great Cat quickly overwhelms the Fantastic Four. However, the team's assailant has greatly underestimated the prowess of the apparently harmless Wyatt Wingfoot.

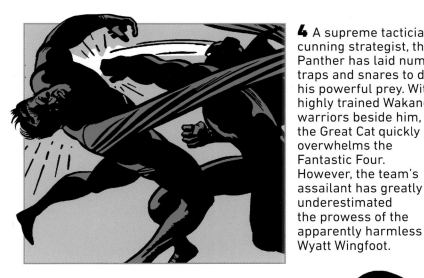

5 While the Black Panther is subduing his super-powered opponents, Wyatt Wingfoot secret infiltrates the Wakandans' command pos and destroys the controls for the Panther's containment traps With the Fantastic Four now free, the tables are swiftly turned...

6 The Black Panther abruptly surrenders. Unmasking himself, he offers a full explanation for his hostile actions, confessing that the entire exercise has been a test of his own fighting abilities. For years, T'Challa has been preparing to confront his greatest enemy—murderous rogue scientist Ulysses Klaw—and had to know that he was fully combat-ready.

MAKING OF A PANTHER

For millennia, each Black Panther is chosen through a series of ritualistic ordeals that have weeded out the unfit and unworthy. The ruling king must accept every challenge for his position and defeat all opponents before being allowed to serve, defend, and represent the Wakandan people.

CHURCH AND STATE

Worship of the Panther God is Wakanda's state religion. The Panther Cult has a strict hierarchy for priests, who must ensure that qualified candidates will replace the incumbent warrior king when he falls. Ranks and designations consist of White Tigers (trainee acolytes), Golden Lions (experienced deacons), Coal Tigers (bishops, ready to take the tests), and Black Panther—the ruling chieftain.

Black Panther (Vol. 3) #62 (Sep. 2003)

THE LAW OF ASCENSION

A Wakandan's Right of Challenge is sacrosanct—a holdover from times when the warrior race's survival depended on the leadership of the best fighter. Bast is always the final arbiter, but in cases where an outcome is unclear or disputed, the High Council of Wakandan chiefs convenes to decide succession. They can apply other tests and their judgment is final.

Black Panther (Vol. 3) #60 (Jul. 2003)

DEMOCRACY IN ACTION

Although Royal Family candidates are trained from birth, all Black Panthers are chosen according to the Rite of Ascension: ordeals any Wakandan can attempt. If triumphant, the newcomer becomes Chieftain of Wakanda and defender of the nation. He or she will enjoy all the physical enhancements that come with Bast's blessing and the wealth and power of the throne.

Black Panther (Vol. 4) #2 (May 2005)

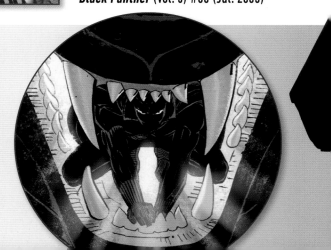

CHOSEN ONE

Every challenger must defeat six warriors before being allowed to battle the ruling Black Panther. After triumphing in the Challenge Ritual, the victor is anointed by priests and wise men with a poultice derived from the sacred heart-shaped herb. This treatment enhances the senses and amplifies the physical attributes of the candidate, who is then judged by the Panther Spirit, Bast. If the candidate survives meeting Bast, he or she retains the physical enhancements and blessing of the Panther God. This transforms a mortal warrior into a superhuman champion with the power, stealth, and agility of an apex predator.

Black Panther (Vol. 4) #2 (May 2005)

SACRED MANTLE

Every Wakandan chieftain since Bashenga has worn royal regalia venerating the Panther God Bast and designed for combat. The Vibranium-laced suit is customized to each Panther's physique and temperament, complementing his or her unique fighting style. Supreme technologist T'Challa continually upgrades his suits, keeping them at the cutting edge of scientific advancement. His modifications also seek the best balance between offensive capability and defensive security.

HEADGEAR

T'Challa's mask contains sophisticated sensors, communications equipment, a direct interface with Wakanda's Kimoyo supercomputer network, and Heads-Up Display systems. Constructed from thousands of interlaced Vibranium modules, this miracle of micro-engineering is mentally activated, instantly forming around the king's head when required.

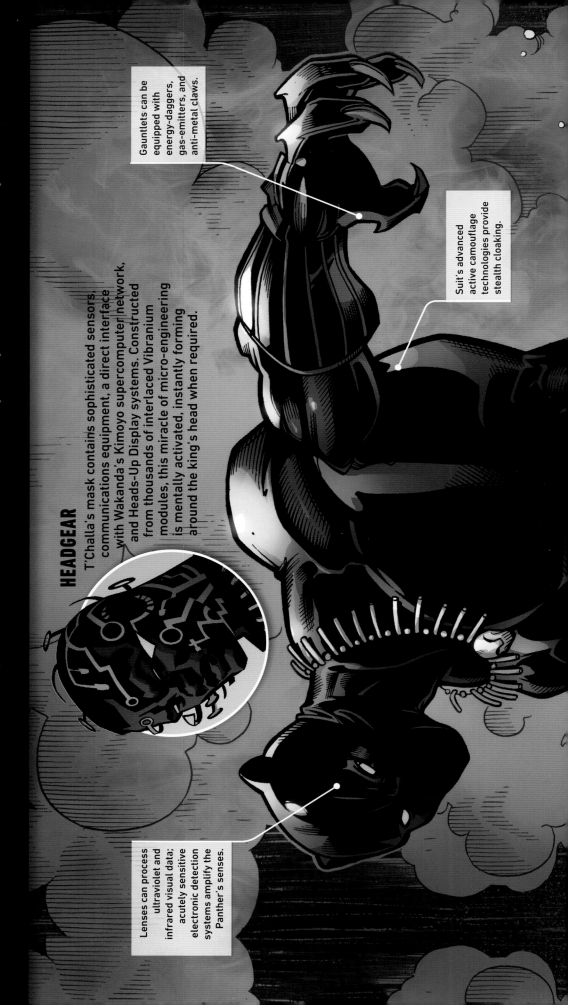

Gauntlets can be equipped with energy-daggers, gas-emitters, and anti-metal claws.

Suit's advanced active camouflage technologies provide stealth cloaking.

Lenses can process ultraviolet and infrared visual data; acutely sensitive electronic detection systems amplify the Panther's senses.

Armor is thought-controlled, partially or fully assembling around the Panther at will.

Vibranium composites in soles and ankles reduce landing impact and noise.

Hard-light shielding is capable of withstanding devastating explosions or a punch from an enraged Hulk.

ARMORED AND DANGEROUS

All Black Panther uniforms are built for battle, but T'Challa constantly reinvents and reworks his suit—striving to handle any possible scenario in an ever-changing, evermore dangerous universe. He has made or adapted specialized gear for specific situations and utilized ancient magic to augment Wakanda's futuristic engineering technologies.

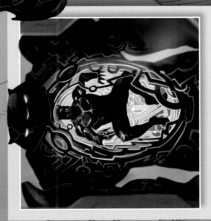

Hulkbuster catsuit
A purpose-built mecha suit, designed specifically to counter the strength and speed of the Incredible Hulk.

Thrice-blessed armor
Mystic battle-gear enhanced with magic spells and force fields to resist any physical threat or supernatural menace.

Space armor
Developed to provide full life-support in the vacuum of space. The suit is impact, temperature, and radiation resistant.

THE BLACK PANTHER DYNASTY

T'Challa is just the latest representative of a warrior-priest tradition stretching back into prehistory. Every Black Panther has been a regal leader and devout Champion of the People, connected to a divine feline patron, and sworn to protect the kingdom from any threat.

> *"The star spirits have given this to us... we must accept it or risk their anger!"*
>
> WAKANDAN WARRIOR

CHANDA

Chanda is King of Wakanda at the start of World War II. In the spirit of neutrality, he offers aid to Colonel Fritz Klaue when the Nazi officer's aircraft crashes in Wakanda. Despite Chanda's friendly overtures, Klaue attempts to secretly take control of the Panther Cult and gain possession of Wakanda's invaluable reserves of Vibranium.

After Klaue kills Chanda's wife Nanali, the chieftain flees into the jungle where a panther throws itself on his knife. Clad in its bloody skin, Chanda accepts the beast's sacrifice and returns to shatter Klaue's dream, before banishing the defeated Nazi from his kingdom forever.

AZZURI THE WISE

Chanda's successor, Azzuri, creates a global spy network that reaches all the way into the White House and even uncovers Captain America's highly classified secret identity. Azzuri carefully balances Wakanda's precious isolationism with a pragmatic understanding that the outer world cannot be forever held at arm's length, and must be carefully monitored.

After repelling an incursion by Nazis intent on appropriating Vibranium for their missile program, Azzuri allies with Sgt. Fury's Howling Commandos and Captain America. Together, they crush a full-scale invasion led by the villainous Red Skull and his superhuman Super-Soldiers Master Man, Warrior Woman, and Tiger Man, who are working with the Wakandan traitor White Gorilla.

BASHENGA

Seeking to protect the ancient, wondrous knowledge of the deity Amun-Ra from the evil Anubis, the Egyptian goddess Bast travels far to find a worthy keeper of the holy secrets. She eventually chooses Wakandan tribal chieftain Bashenga for the honor, anointing his face with her sacred mark. Bashenga is already a great leader, having trained his tribe to battle mutants created by radiation from the mound of meteoric mineral his descendants come to call Vibranium.

A wise and mighty king, Bashenga creates the sacred Panther robes in Bast's honor. The robes are worn by all who follow in his footsteps, while his war-spear passes down from chieftain to chieftain, becoming a symbol of divine authority to Wakandans.

T'CHAKA, THE GREAT ISOLATIONIST

Azzuri's first-born son, T'Chaka, rules Wakanda for decades, methodically guiding his people toward becoming a modern technological nation. At the same time, he strives to honor the spiritual connection to the Panther guardian and Africa's old ways of magic, as championed by the sorcerer Zawavari.

An isolationist fiercely proud of Wakanda's heritage, T'Chaka nevertheless adopts a white orphan named Hunter. After his first wife N'Yami dies giving birth to their son, T'Challa, T'Chaka marries an "outworlder"—a South African named Ramonda. Another son, Jakarra, is born out of wedlock before Ramonda bears him a female heir, Shuri.

T'Chaka is assassinated by Ulysses Klaw during the villain's failed attempt to seize Wakanda's Vibranium. He is avenged by his son T'Challa and succeeded by his brother S'Yan.

S'YAN THE FAST

Scholarly S'Yan is Azzuri's second son. After his brother T'Chaka is murdered, he reluctantly takes part in the trials to become the next Black Panther. His great speed and strength earns him the nickname "S'Yan the Fast." Working beside chief administrator N'Baza, S'Yan serves as Chieftain of Wakanda while T'Challa is schooled abroad. Never comfortable with the role, S'Yan is grateful when the Orphan Prince returns to defeat him in the ritual Black Panther tournament and takes back the throne.

S'Yan goes on to serve for years as an elder statesman, diplomat, ambassador, and close advisor to T'Challa. He perishes saving the Queen Mother Ramonda from Doctor Doom's forces during the Latverian attack on Wakanda.

SHURI

Headstrong and privileged, T'Chaka and Ramonda's daughter, Shuri, yearns to rule as a Black Panther. She achieves her heart's desire after abandoning personal ambition and embracing the responsibility of leadership and self-sacrifice. After giving her life to save her brother T'Challa, Shuri mystically evolves into a new spiritual totem for the Wakandan people.

ORIGIN

Like all children of the Royal Family, Princess Shuri is rigorously trained in martial arts from an early age. She has long wanted to be the Black Panther, but loses out on the role to her older brother, T'Challa. Shuri's failure prompts years of frivolous behavior until the day the U.S. masterminds an invasion of Wakanda, and she tastes real combat for the first time.

When T'Challa falls to the villainous Doctor Doom, the Panther Spirit tests Shuri, but deems her unworthy. Deciding to die fighting totem-eater Morlun, Shuri earns Bast's blessing by finally putting Wakanda before her own ambitions. Shuri governs through the nation's darkest hours, and dies heroically when Namor's Cabal takes over. With her body imprisoned in an amber trap, Shuri is eventually resurrected by T'Challa and returns as a mystically empowered avatar.

> ### "You've faced the muscle of Wakanda...now face its claws."
> SHURI

Killer queen
Shuri quickly rises to the challenge of rule, aggressively fortifying Wakanda and creating a new secret service branch, P.R.I.D.E. (Princess Regent Intelligence Division Executives). She fiercely pursues national enemies such as Doctor Doom and Namor the Sub-Mariner, and foils a world-domination plot by her country's greatest nemesis, Klaw. However, her valiant reign ends when Namor's Cabal invades and she sacrifices herself to save T'Challa.

Going underground
When hostile foreign powers orchestrate a superhuman invasion of Wakanda, Shuri is trapped in the Vibranium mine with the murderous Radioactive Man. The Super Villain has been hired by Americans seeking to destroy Wakanda's economy by using his atomic powers to make the miraculous mineral inert. Shuri takes her first steps towards true regal responsibility and authority by killing Radioactive Man with the Ebony Blade before his attack can succeed.

GUARDIAN SPIRIT

After years of craving power, Shuri learns its great cost as she defends the Wakandan people from increasingly catastrophic assaults. While her brother, T'Challa, largely embraces the Panther God's aspect of wisdom, Shuri favors the deity's ruthless pursuit of justice. With her nation continually under siege, the young queen quickly develops into a resolute avenger of wrongs perpetrated against her country and a mighty defender of Wakandan lives and values.

Shuri's new attire acknowledges that other deities exist beside Bast, the Panther Spirit.

Unlike her brother T'Challa, Shuri now values ancient weapons over modern technology.

Shuri's wooden staff denotes a resolute path toward peace and wisdom.

DATA FILE

FIRST APPEARANCE: *Black Panther* (Vol. 4) #2 (May 2005)

OCCUPATION: Black Panther, Princess Regent, Queen

AFFILIATIONS: Panther Cult, Wakandan School for Alternative Studies, P.R.I.D.E. (Princess Regent Intelligence Division Executives)

POWERS/ABILITIES: Speed, agility, strength, reflexes, and senses enhanced by the heart-shaped herb; ability to change to flexible stone; animorphism; access to all the lore and history of Wakanda

BASE: Wakanda

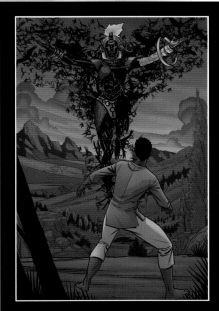

Aja Adana

Shuri is reborn as an all-wise shapeshifter possessing the knowledge of countless generations. She acts decisively in the three-way war between T'Challa's forces, the People's revolutionaries, and the women's protective movement known as the Midnight Angels. Her enhanced grasp of history and human nature compels Shuri—as the "Aja Adana" (Ancient Future)—to fight ferociously for her people. These new abilities later allow her to play peacemaker, forging new ways forward for all of Wakanda's factions.

Stranger in town

When Ramonda returns to Wakanda, T'Challa delights in showing her the scientific marvels he has created. However, his stepmother is far more concerned with how he deals with the country's first influx of drug-runners and narcotics abusers. As a former captive herself, Ramonda advocates a therapeutic approach with counseling, rather than T'Challa's hardline incarceration of addicts such as the Royal Family's ward, Kantu.

All in the family

After years of patiently holding her tongue, Ramonda confronts T'Challa and demands that her stepson address his responsibilities to the kingdom by settling the issue of succession. Her wise counsel persuades T'Challa to begin a global search of suitable and willing candidates to become his queen. The quest results in the Black Panther marrying his childhood sweetheart Ororo Munroe, now the mutant Super Hero Storm.

TRIBAL ELDER

A large proportion of Ramonda's royal duties involve the *Dora Milaje*. This women-only royal bodyguard corps represents all 18 tribes that make up the Wakandan people. Operating under strict protocols and laws, they hold themselves to ethical standards far above that of ordinary citizens.

As Queen Mother, Ramonda acts as advisor, judge, and final arbiter in all matters of policy, which regretfully compels her to uphold a death sentence on the accused murderer and *Dora Milaje* officer, Captain Aneka.

DATA FILE

FIRST APPEARANCE: *Marvel Comics Presents* (Vol. 1) #14 (Mar. 1989)

OCCUPATION: Queen, politician

AFFILIATIONS: Taifa Ngao, Wakandan Royal Family

BASE: Birnin Zana, Wakanda

Ramonda wears simple clothes, preferring to be with, not above, the people.

A simple staff is the enduring symbol of all Wakandan royalty.

Ramonda stays connected to Wakanda's data-net through the Kimoyo beads freely given to every citizen.

When Queen N'Yami dies giving birth to T'Challa, bereaved King T'Chaka controversially marries an outworlder: South African princess Ramonda. The family is happy and grows larger after Ramonda gives birth to a daughter, Shuri.

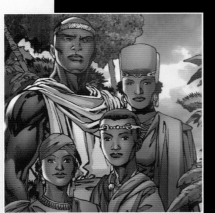

However, when T'Challa is still very young, Ramonda abruptly vanishes. Abducted by South African politician Anton Pretorius—who has developed an all-consuming obsession with her—Ramonda spends the next 30 years as his slave, while her loved ones tragically believe she has abandoned them.

Ramonda is eventually rescued by her stepson T'Challa, who reinstates her as Wakanda's Queen Mother. As such she is invested with a considerable degree of autonomous power as matriarch of the nation.

*"I will meet you head on. Don't **expect any less** from me."*

QUEEN MOTHER RAMONDA

Mother knows best

After Doctor Doom incapacitates T'Challa, Ramonda overturns the king's edicts banning sorcerers and transports her dying stepson to the exiled shaman Zawavari. While the mage attempts to resurrect T'Challa, the Queen Mother—at Queen Ororo's urging—asks her own daughter, Shuri, to undergo the rite of the heart-shaped herb and become Wakanda's Commander-in-Chief: the next Black Panther.

QUEEN MOTHER RAMONDA

Quietly competent, compassionate, and forceful, Ramonda is a potent power behind the Wakandan throne. She offers great wisdom gained from a life experiencing the most exalted as well as the most degrading positions in society. She also acts an effective bridge between the old ways of traditional Wakanda and the technological advances initiated by T'Challa.

ORIGIN

The "Adored Ones" stem from an ancient tradition in which each of the Wakandan confederation's 18 tribes submit a potential wife for the king. The coveted position of Bride-in-Training eventually becomes highly political. Contemporary Black Panthers realize that by favoring any one bride-offering over all the others, they risk creating anger and dissent among the ever-quarreling tribes.

Modern kings like T'Challa regard the gesture and role as purely symbolic. Candidate brides are instead schooled in all aspects of military accomplishment and trained as elite bodyguards and troubleshooters for the Royal Family.

> "We fight together, we work together, we learn together, and we love together."
>
> CAPTAIN ANEKA

Duty

The best and brightest—or sometimes the most difficult and unruly—maidens are chosen to represent their tribes and dispatched to the Upanga training center in Birnin Zana. Here, they are transformed into the most potent, patriotic, and feared soldiers in Wakanda. They learn various skills—from unarmed combat to court etiquette—to present the monarch in the best light.

Devotion

Being a *Dora Milaje* is a lifelong commitment. When infant princess Ce'Athauna Asira Davin is exiled to Chicago to quell unrest in her Jabari homeland, an Adored One goes with her, masquerading as her grandmother. She raises the princess as Chanté Giovanni Brown (Queen Divine Justice) at the order of the Black Panther, until the day Chanté will also become a *Dora Milaje*.

Honor

Trained as warriors utterly loyal to Wakanda, many *Dora Milaje* feel betrayed by T'Challa's failure to protect the nation and save his sister Shuri from Namor's Cabal. During the People's revolution, many defect to the cause of rebel Midnight Angels Ayo and Aneka. They dedicate their lives to defending oppressed women subjugated by opportunistic regional tribal leaders who seek power for themselves.

DORA MILAJE

The members of the *Dora Milaje* are chaste and untouchable: brides-in-waiting forbidden all romantic liaisons because they are symbolically pledged to the king. Instead, the "Adored Ones" are trained as his ultimate bodyguards—symbols of his wealth and power, as well as his last line of defense.

PRIDE AND EDUCATION

Dora Milaje are proud, formidable Wakandan women, fanatical unto death in defending their king. They are instilled with a strict code of honor: "To serve, to fight, to be fierce, to be fearless." Highly educated, their schooling includes learning many different languages, although by tradition they are only permitted to speak to the king in African Hausa (a language unknown to ordinary Wakandans). From their first day at Upanga, Adored Ones learn all aspects of warfare, including strategy, chemistry, and electronics.

Every *Dora Milaje* is trained in the use of many weapons, ancient and modern.

Personalized tribal markings denote individual status and achievement.

Dora Milaje adjust their outfits to suit different situations, always ensuring they are dressed to kill.

Sacrifice

When Doctor Doom breaks a truce and attempts to kill T'Challa during a negotiation, the Black Panther's *Dora Milaje* spring into action against the most evil man alive. Without a second thought, one of them sacrifices herself to hold the villain at bay, allowing her companion-in-arms to get the grievously wounded King T'Challa to safety.

DATA FILE

FIRST APPEARANCE: *Black Panther* (Vol. 3) #1 (Nov. 1998)

OCCUPATION: Royal bodyguards, Brides-in-Training (traditional and honorary role)

AIMS: Defense of Black Panther and Royal Family

AFFILIATIONS: Royal Family

POWERS/ABILITIES: Martial arts and espionage training; experts with all weapons and ordnance; advanced surveillance techniques

BASE: Upanga, Birnin Zana, Wakanda

SOUND AND FURY

Transformed into living sound, Klaw is invulnerable and virtually immortal. However, his metamorphosis causes radical personality shifts. Whenever he resurfaces, opponents cannot be sure if he will be a complete fool, ferocious flunky for hire, or a cunning mastermind with schemes to conquer or destroy humanity. One thing never changes: Klaw's hatred of T'Challa and unshakable hunger to kill every costumed hero who ever stands in his way.

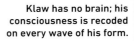

Klaw has no brain; his consciousness is recoded on every wave of his form.

Master of Evil

After his defeats by the Fantastic Four, Klaw becomes a super-powered criminal and mercenary, fighting for profit either alone or with equally notorious villains. Whether battling in Ultron's Masters of Evil, the Wizard's Frightful Four, or leading his own Fearsome Foursome, the result of his vindictive endeavors is always the same—he suffers humiliating defeat at the hands of heroes he considers his inferiors.

The sound converter is Klaw's greatest weapon, but also the most vulnerable point for attack.

DATA FILE

AL NAME: Ulysses Klaw

FIRST APPEARANCE: (As human criminal) *Fantastic Four* (Vol. 1) #53 (Aug.1966); (As living sound being) *Fantastic Four* (Vol. 1) #56 (Nov. 1966)

OCCUPATION: Scientist, criminal, conqueror

AFFILIATIONS: A.I.M., Intelligencia, Frightful Four, Masters of Evil, Fearsome Foursome

POWERS/ABILITIES: Body made of solidified sound; sonic converter prosthetic generates sonic blasts, hypnotizes, and forms solid-sound constructs

Bad vibrations

Restored to peak efficiency, Klaw plans to disgrace Wakanda and kill T'Challa. His complex scheme involves fomenting war with Priest-lord Ghaur's Deviants and framing Wakanda for destroying U.S. warships. Eventually, an impatient Klaw betrays his silent partner Hunter—the White Wolf—and goes on a titanic rampage, possessing tidal waves and subway trains in his haste to kill the Panther.

The compacted sound body is impervious to attack and can only be disrupted by Vibranium.

ORIGIN

Ruthless rogue scientist Ulysses Klaw invades Wakanda to obtain Vibranium, killing Black Panther T'Chaka and taking many slaves in the process. Heartbroken but defiant, the young Prince T'Challa drives off the occupying force with the invader's own sonic converter weapon. During the final battle, the defeated mastermind's right hand is destroyed.

Several years later, Klaw stages a second attempt to conquer Wakanda with improved sonic-powered weapons and solid-sound monsters. Crushed by the Fantastic Four and the recently anointed Black Panther, T'Challa, Klaw hurls himself into his main sonic converter. The heroes believe him dead, but the deranged genius has himself been transformed into a creature of solid, sentient sound.

> *"Thus, does the **Master of Sound** exact his final revenge!"*
>
> KLAW

M.U.S.I.C. Maestro

After Shuri becomes the Black Panther, Klaw attempts his most daring scheme: blackmailing A.I.M. scientists into using new sound-based lifeform M.U.S.I.C. (Multiframe Universal Sonic Integration Codec) to subjugate every mind on Earth. Thwarted by Shuri's coalition of Super Heroes—Ka-Zar, Shanna, Wolverine, and Spider-Man— Klaw is blasted into space when Black Widow and the Black Panther invade his orbiting satellite headquarters.

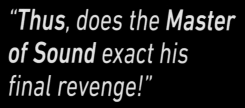

KLAW

A malign genius composed of self-generated sound waves, Ulysses Klaw loses what little humanity he has after becoming a sentient, vindictive mass of vibrations. All that drives him now is greed, hatred of humanity, and a remorseless determination to punish Wakanda for his own sins.

ORIGIN

During World War II's darkest days, Steve Rogers is remade into the ultimate fighting machine by a Super-Soldier Serum. As Captain America he becomes democracy's Sentinel of Liberty. Working with partner Bucky Barnes and super-teams such as the Invaders, "Cap" tirelessly combats terror and oppression, but is presumed lost in the last days of the war.

Decades later, he is recovered from a block of Arctic ice by the Avengers. A revived Captain America returns to duty, saving the country and the world from all manner of danger. In the course of his neverending war against evil and injustice, Captain America becomes the most respected and trusted Super Hero of all. However, in his heart, Steve Rogers knows he is only a man doing his best to safeguard freedom and justice.

African nightmare

Decades after fighting beside Black Panther Azzuri, a resuscitated Captain America meets a second Black Panther. King T'Challa asks the hero to help Wakanda battle a resurrected Baron Zemo and destroy a world-threatening death-ray satellite. Although the villain turns out to be an impostor, the danger is real, and, in the explosive aftermath, the Star-Spangled Sentinel suggests that the Black Panther take his place in the Avengers.

> *"I'm no more a hero than **any** man who fights for **justice** and **freedom** and **brotherhood**!"*
>
> CAPTAIN AMERICA

CAPTAIN AMERICA

The foremost defender of freedom, democracy, and American values, super-soldier Steve Rogers is humanity's most ardent protector. An indomitable warrior, Captain America has inspired and trained generations of Super Heroes in how to be the perfect hero.

Safari showdown

Soon after the U.S. enters World War II, Captain America is sent to Africa, where he encounters Black Panther Azzuri. Initially the two heroes battle each other to a standstill, but finally unite against and defeat an army of Nazi invaders. Having earned each other's great respect during combat, these national symbols of justice part as sworn comrades. Captain America returns home with a sample of Vibranium that will make his next shield a supreme defensive weapon.

ALL-AMERICAN IDOL

Greater than all of his enhanced physical abilities, or the cutting-edge ordnance and defenses supplied by U.S. military technicians, is Steve Rogers' unflagging spirit. His quick-fire strategic skills and tactical ingenuity, combined with a never-surrender attitude make him a truly formidable opponent and a match for any enemy.

Distinctive headgear allows complete sensory input, while providing full protection from injury.

The latest shield has an energy blade and can be divided into two sections.

Body armor is highly impact-resistant, but light and supple enough to allow free movement.

The end times

During the incursions of alternate universes, a depowered Steve Rogers quits Black Panther's Illuminati group because of its proposed immoral actions—destroying other Earths to save its own. With a S.H.I.E.L.D.-sponsored Avengers team, Rogers hunts T'Challa and his former allies across the world, resolving to get justice for the countless deaths they have caused. Fighting to his last breath, he seemingly dies with the multiverse.

DATA FILE

REAL NAME: Steven "Steve" Grant Rogers

FIRST APPEARANCE: (Golden Age) *Captain America Comics* (Vol. 1) #1 (Mar. 1941); (Silver Age) *The Avengers* (Vol. 1) #4 (Mar. 1964)

OCCUPATION: Soldier, adventurer, federal official, intelligence operative

AFFILIATIONS: Avengers, Invaders, S.H.I.E.L.D., Secret Avengers, Illuminati

POWERS/ABILITIES: Chemically enhanced human soldier; supreme gymnast and martial artist; brilliant combat tactician and strategist

ATTENTION SEEKING

Possessing an astute grasp of human nature, Killmonger uses his tremendous physique to intimidate everybody he meets. This tactic is reinforced by his grandiose manner of speech, flamboyantly barbaric style of dress, and the exotic weaponry he wears. All these combine to give him a psychological advantage. His every move shouts: "Don't mess with me if you want to live."

Back from the dead

Killmonger's frequent use of the mystical Resurrection Altar to cheat death eventually causes the veil between the realms of Life and Death to fray. After the members of his fanatical Death Regiments sacrifice themselves to revive Killmonger once more, mystic master Doctor Voodoo places temporal locks on the Resurrection Altar to stop the spiritual rot.

Skull symbols signify to his enemies that Killmonger has conquered death many times.

DATA FILE

REAL NAME: Erik Killmonger (formerly N'Jadaka)

FIRST APPEARANCE: *Jungle Action* (Vol. 2) #6 (Sep. 1973)

OCCUPATION: Tribal leader, revolutionary, despot

AFFILIATIONS: Dictator of Niganda, Black Panther

POWERS/ABILITIES: Enhanced strength, speed, durability, and senses derived from a synthetic version of heart-shaped herb

BASE: Harlem, New York City; N'Jadaka village, Wakanda

Lethal legacy

Secretly sponsored by American intelligence agencies, Killmonger conquers Wakanda's neighbor, the territory of Niganda, and again attempts to destroy T'Challa. He is killed by the Panther's ally Monica Rambeau, but leaves behind an army of well-armed, devout followers, led by his numerous children, who have all pledged to continue his bloody work.

Through science and training, Erik has turned his body into a lethal, muscle-bound weapon.

Every aspect of attire is designed to terrify opponents, while also concealing armaments.

ORIGIN

Captured during Klaw's invasion of Wakanda, N'Jadaka is unjustly banished after T'Chaka's murder. Raised in Harlem, New York City, he overcomes extreme poverty to graduate from the prestigious Massachusetts Institute of Technology with a business degree and an engineering PhD. Hungry to tear down the regime and country he feels has abandoned him, N'Jadaka boosts his physique with a synthetic version of the heart-shaped herb, before tricking T'Challa into allowing him to return to his native Wakanda. Taking the name Erik Killmonger, N'Jadaka gathers together an army of psychopaths and disillusioned Wakandans. Despite his charisma, however, his ruthlessness divides his followers. Many desert Killmonger's cause, while others regard him as a saint; even reviving him on the arcane Resurrection Altar after he is killed by T'Challa.

"Your father was not fit to be king...and neither are you!"

ERIK KILLMONGER

Usurpers Assemble

While waging economic war on Wakanda, Killmonger forces T'Challa to participate in ritual combat. After a long and brutal battle—and thanks to a fortunate distraction—Killmonger wins and becomes the new Black Panther. While T'Challa recovers from his near-fatal injuries, Killmonger returns to the U.S. and demands to take his defeated enemy's place in the Avengers.

KILLMONGER

T'Challa's archenemy is an exiled Wakandan who believes he can do a far better job of ruling the African nation. Through sheer determination and mastery of science, N'Jadaka transforms himself into Erik Killmonger, a truly fearsome warrior who is the Black Panther's superior—and not even death can deter Killmonger from his mission.

FANTASTIC FOUR

The Fantastic Four are the world's greatest heroes. They have stopped all-conquering villains, saved universes, and roamed across dimensions and time. They also act as guides and ambassadors for super-powered allies, such as the Avengers, the Inhumans, and Black Panther.

Render unto Caesar
When they first meet, T'Challa attacks the team to test his own abilities, and their subsequent battle together against the villain Klaw cements a lifelong friendship. Many shared adventures follow, including their memorable joint investigation of a power anomaly on Wakanda's border. Here they unearth an imperial Roman city held in stasis by Gaius Tiberius Augustus Agrippa—a Roman soldier maintaining his city's timeless state with energies from a crashed alien starship.

> *"The human spirit can **never** truly be conquered!"*
>
> REED RICHARDS

Human Torch (Johnny Storm)

Mister Fantastic (Reed Richards)

Thing (Ben Grimm)

Invisible Woman (Susan Richards)

DATA FILE

FIRST APPEARANCE: *Fantastic Four* (Vol. 1) #1 (Nov. 1961)

OCCUPATION: Adventurers, explorers

AFFILIATIONS: Avengers, Illuminati, X-Men, S.H.I.E.L.D.

POWERS/ABILITIES: Cosmic ray mutations resulting in: elastic body (Mister Fantastic); increased strength and durability (Thing), invisible energy manipulation (Invisible Woman); and pyrokinetic control (Human Torch)

ORIGIN

Scientist Reed Richards, pilot Ben Grimm, Reed's girlfriend Sue Storm, and her teenaged brother Johnny take a test star-craft into space. The ship has insufficient shielding, and they are permanently transformed by cosmic radiation. Surviving their unsanctioned voyage, the four bold companions gain astounding powers that they pledge to use to battle injustice, thwart planetary threats, and benefit mankind. Over years of valiant service, they have become foremost among Earth's Super Heroes, but at heart are always more a family than a team. They quarrel, split up, or take on new members, but always reunite, ever ready to face the uncanny and unknown.

DATA FILE

REAL NAME: Matthew Murdock

FIRST APPEARANCE: *Daredevil* (Vol. 1) #1 (Apr. 1964)

OCCUPATION: Adventurer, vigilante, law attorney

AFFILIATIONS: Avengers, Defenders, the Hand

POWERS/ABILITIES: Radiation-induced hyper-senses, "radar sense," martial artist, acrobat

BASE: Hell's Kitchen, New York City; San Francisco, California

ORIGIN

Young Matt Murdock saves an old man from a truck transporting radioactive waste. The impact of a loose canister blinds the boy forever, but amplifies his other senses and creates a unique "radar sense." Although Matt's prize-fighter father, "Battlin' Jack" Murdock, wishes him to avoid violence and study to be a lawyer, young Murdock secretly trains in acrobatics and studies martial arts. When his father is murdered, a grieving Matt creates the costumed identity of Daredevil to avenge his death. After completing his mission, Matt continues the masked role, bringing the guilty to book and seeking justice for the disadvantaged—just as he does in his civilian life as a celebrated defense attorney.

"Here comes Daredevil...
*the **Man without Fear**!"*

DAREDEVIL

The all-purpose billy club is a highly effective, versatile, and non-lethal weapon.

The red devil motif has a terrifying psychological impact on Daredevil's prey.

A friend in need

Daredevil and the Black Panther first meet when the sightless champion battles Starr Saxon, a deranged enemy who knows his true identity. Concealing his vigilante alter ego is vital to a hero who is a legally-appointed officer of the court in his civilian guise. To help throw off suspicion, T'Challa often masquerades as Daredevil, even replacing his comrade as guardian of Hell's Kitchen if the need ever arises.

DAREDEVIL

Fearless and driven, Daredevil pursues a tireless, two-tiered crusade for justice. He defends citizens' rights as a brilliant trial lawyer in court and as a masked protector on the mean streets of Hell's Kitchen in the city he loves, New York.

THE AVENGERS

When T'Challa relocates to the U.S., he joins the constantly changing ranks of the Avengers, Earth's Mightiest Heroes. Battling world-shattering threats and more insidious menaces, the Black Panther becomes particularly close to some of his valiant comrades.

THE WASP

Although Janet van Dyne gained wings, bio-stings, and size-shifting powers from her sometimes-husband Dr. Henry Pym, her greatest abilities are her incredible leadership and organizational skills. These—along with a canny eye for combat tactics and strategy—make The Wasp one of the most effective chairpersons in the Avengers' long and illustrious history.

THE VISION

A solar-powered, density-shifting synthezoid, the Vision is an artificial being patterned on World War II hero the Human Torch. Reprogrammed by the evil robot Ultron-5, the Vision initially attacks the Avengers, but T'Challa and the team uncover his true origins, liberating his consciousness. Despite the Vision's synthetic makeup, he emerges as one of the Avengers' most sensitive and highly intuitive members, as well as one of the most powerful.

HAWKEYE

Former circus performer Clint Barton uses his unerring aim, specialized hi-tech arrows, and expert combat training provided by Captain America to flamboyantly fight injustice as the hero Hawkeye. Thanks to a borrowed Pym Particle growth serum, Clint also occasionally goes into action as a second Goliath.

BLACK KNIGHT

Dane Whitman is a respected scientist descended from a long line of heroes tainted by sorcery that dates back to the time of King Arthur. As the Black Knight, Dane combines hi-tech weaponry with the accursed Ebony Blade. When Dane succumbs to the corrupting influence of the curse, the sword falls into the hands of the Vatican, but is later confiscated by the Black Panther after it is used to attack Wakanda.

IRON MAN

Billionaire inventor Tony Stark creates Iron Man armor to prolong his life. He later repurposes it, perpetually adding weapons and new technology to the outfit to become one of the most powerful Super Heroes on Earth. Strong-willed and domineering, Stark's respect for the Black Panther is tempered by a compulsive competitive streak that frequently boils over into confrontation.

THOR

The immortal Thunder God of Asgard has fought evil and slain monsters for centuries, but considers the indomitable mortals of the Avengers among his greatest allies and comrades. Thor has a special affinity with the Black Panther, a fellow scion of a royal line trying to adjust to a culture and world so very different from his wondrous homeland.

ANT-MAN / GOLIATH / YELLOWJACKET / GIANT-MAN

Biochemist Dr. Henry Pym is a founding member of the Avengers and uses his scientific brilliance to become a succession of size-changing heroes. However, he is never truly at ease in the role of a costumed adventurer. Although his intellect and education are equal to T'Challa's, he is less able to cope with the unrelenting pressure of constant danger.

Fish out of water

Amicable relations between Super Hero monarchs break down after T'Challa catches his soldiers selling advanced Wakandan weapons to Atlantis. An ultimately futile attempt to peacefully resolve the problem with Namor escalates into a brutal clash of kings—and an exchange of missiles. Thankfully, Doctor Strange and the Defenders expose the true wrongdoers and prevent a devastating war between the hidden kingdoms.

ORIGIN

In the early 20th century, a boy is born of a union between polar explorer Leonard McKenzie and Princess Fen of Atlantis. Possessing mighty powers, he can live both above and beneath the sea. Bred to hate humanity, Prince Namor is originally a scourge of mankind, but softens his position after meeting New York policewoman, Betty Dean.

During World War II, Sub-Mariner serves briefly as a surface-world Super Hero, but eventually he vanishes from sight. He is later found and revived from an amnesiac state by the Human Torch, Johnny Storm.

For years, Namor alternates as both threat and hero. He will always act to safeguard Earth's oceans and sub-sea denizens and, when interests overlap, save humanity from deadly menaces and its own collective greed.

"Imperius Rex!"

NAMOR

Conscience of the king

When the members of the Illuminati are finally compelled to destroy an alternate Earth to save their own, none of the heroes can bring themselves to detonate the antimatter bomb. With seconds to spare and despising his weak, ethical allies, Namor triggers the device and murders billions of innocents to save his own subjects and the world they inhabit. The shock of his desperate actions shatters Namor's spirit.

NAMOR
THE SUB-MARINER

One of the most powerful beings on Earth, Namor has been many things in his time: a monarch, a villain, an outcast, and a hero. Rejecting all labels, he considers himself to be someone driven by necessity to do what is right for his people and his planet. If that means eliminating allies as well as enemies, so be it!

Sub-Mariner's eyesight can penetrate sub-sea murk, silt, or darkness.

Namor's gills allow him to extract oxygen from water at any depth.

DATA FILE

REAL NAME: Namor McKenzie

FIRST APPEARANCE: (Golden Age) *Motion Picture Funnies Weekly* (Vol. 1) #1 (Apr. 1941); (Silver Age) *Fantastic Four* (Vol. 1) #4 (May 1962)

OCCUPATION: King of Atlantis, adventurer, warrior, commando

AFFILIATIONS: The Cabal, X-Men, Illuminati, Avengers, Invaders

POWERS/ABILITIES: Amphibious physiological adaptation; super-strength, speed, reflexes, durability, flight, bioelectrical generation

BASE: Atlantis

STORMY SEA LORD

Apparently ageless, immeasurably powerful, and ruler of a vast and mighty nation, Namor the Sub-Mariner has never learned to compromise or act cooperatively. Although a member of several Super Hero teams and alliances over the decades, he always puts his own opinions and the welfare of his people before all other considerations. This unwillingness to negotiate frequently leads to catastrophic clashes with his closest friends and allies.

Regal clothing is based on a moisture-preserving suit designed by Reed Richards.

Strange bedfellows

Namor is the ultimate outsider, as much foe as friend to humanity, but he feels a special kinship with those he regards as fellow rulers. When interests align, Sub-Mariner will act as a neutral negotiator in state matters between T'Challa and former enemies like Magneto or Doctor Doom. On one occasion, Namor's guarantee leads to betrayal when Doctor Doom savagely attacks the Black Panther, triggering a Battle Royal.

HOUND OF HELL

Hunter truly loves Wakanda, but can only see issues on his own terms. He always believes he knows what is best for the country and its people.

After being exiled by T'Challa, Hunter takes his Dogs of War with him to New York City. He establishes them as a supreme mercenary force for sale to foreign governments, as well as using them as a way of keeping an eye on Wakanda's potential enemies.

Helmet contains numerous Wakandan surveillance devices, sensors, and communications systems.

Big brother is watching
As T'Challa grows up, he discovers the terrible things his older brother has done in the name of Wakanda. Refusing to believe their father knows this, the young boy challenges Hunter and realizes that despite all his easy rationalizations, the White Wolf commits atrocities because he likes causing pain and being in control.

DATA FILE

REAL NAME: Hunter

FIRST APPEARANCE: *Black Panther* (Vol. 3) #4 (Feb. 1999)

OCCUPATION: Espionage agent, mercenary terrorist

AFFILIATIONS: *Hatut Zeraze* ("Dogs of War"), Wakandan Royal Family

POWERS/ABILITIES: Ordinary human trained to optimum in killing disciplines; espionage; access to Wakanda's advanced technology and weaponry

BASE: Mobile

Scheming Wolf

To punish international espionage conclave XCon for inciting a coup in Wakanda, Hunter instigates a complex scheme to eradicate the organization from within. The opening gambit involves allying himself with his nation's greatest enemy, Klaw, in a pact to destroy the Black Panther. The wily White Wolf knows this will distract T'Challa long enough for him to do what is necessary.

Justice is served

Hunter is utterly devoted to his *Hatut Zeraze*, as they are to him. When deranged *Dora Milaje* Nakia (Malice II) kills some of them, Hunter strongly urges T'Challa to prosecute her for murder and is enraged when his wishes are ignored. As always, the White Wolf does what he wants, justifying it as being in the national interest.

Uniform is laced with bulletproof, shock-negating Vibranium.

When his parents die in a plane crash, Hunter is taken into the Wakandan Royal Household and raised by King T'Chaka and Queen N'Yami as a son. When T'Challa is born, a resentful Hunter realizes that as a white European, he will never be T'Chaka's heir and pushes himself to become the greatest warrior he possibly can. After T'Chaka appoints Hunter head of the *Hatut Zeraze*, the "White Wolf" constantly abuses his power by targeting political dissidents, always justifying his actions as necessary for the defense of Wakanda. When Killmonger defeats T'Challa in ritual combat and briefly assumes the position of Wakanda's Black Panther, Hunter—despite despising his stepbrother— offers to quietly assassinate the usurper and cannot understand why the offer is refused.

> *"It is time to show you who is the true son of Wakanda."*
>
> **HUNTER**

Brought to heel

When Shuri becomes Black Panther and queen of Wakanda, T'Challa moves to the U.S. and Hunter follows. On arrival he challenges T'Challa by strangling three women the 'panther vigilante' had previously rescued as the protector of Hell's Kitchen. Seeking a final showdown with his hated brother, Hunter is forced to finally and painfully concede that T'Challa will always be the better man.

HUNTER
THE WHITE WOLF

Smart, charming, debonair, and utterly devoid of conscience, the White Wolf is the ultimate superspy. Employing Wakanda's incredible arsenal of weapons and resources, he wanders the globe like a ghost, mercilessly destroying those who threaten his vision for his adopted homeland. That ideology applies as much to friends, allies, and family, as it does to sworn enemies.

CHANGAMIRE

Wakanda is a land of warriors and wonders, but often the most powerful forces that shape a nation stem from less glamorous sources. Studious scholars and gentle questioners can sometimes bring about greater—or more dangerous—change than any king or hero.

Agent of change

Wracked with guilt that his teachings could be so deeply misunderstood and cause violence, Changamire abandons neutrality and makes an impassioned plea to those Wakandans destroying their own nation. His broadcast—universally watched from each citizen's Kimoyo beads—breaks empath Zenzi's emotion-controlling spell, depriving the People of half their forces. This allows T'Challa's defenders to end the conflict. Changamire then acts as arbiter and advisor as the Black Panther reforms the way Wakanda is governed.

Kimoyo beads keep the elderly educator in touch with the attitudes of the young.

Changamire treasures the power of words, but knows ideas must be shaped by one's actions.

"Who, in full sanity, would try to hold a nation under their feet?"

CHANGAMIRE

ORIGIN

During the reign of King T'Chaka, young professor Changamire is invited with a select group of other thinkers to join the Royal Court and share their ideas. He grows close to new queen Ramonda while tutoring her, but his anti-monarchical views cause concern and he is banished from Birnin Zana. Returning to the Hekima Shulē in Birnin Azzaria (City of Knowledge) he settles into a prestigious career as a venerated educator, enlightening generations of young minds. One of these is self-appointed prophet Tetu, who passionately embraces Changamire's message of self-determination—but chooses to ignore his mentor's respect for life and other people's opinions.

DATA FILE

FIRST APPEARANCE: *Black Panther* (Vol. 6) #2 (Jul. 2016)

OCCUPATION: Educator, philosopher

AFFILIATIONS: Hekima Shulē, Birnin Azzaria

POWERS/ABILITIES: Deeply ethical and highly persuasive thinker

BASE: Birnin Azzaria, Wakanda

Perhaps evolving from the spy-ring created by Azzuri the Wise during World War II to monitor foreign governments, the *Hatut Zeraze* is officially convened in T'Chaka's reign. It soon grows into a dreaded secret police force, ferreting out perceived treason at home and threats beyond the nation's borders. It achieves autonomy under S'Yan after T'Challa's adopted brother, Hunter the White Wolf, takes control.

Disbanded by T'Challa, the Dogs of War, as they are known, go underground, repurposed by Hunter as a mercenary squad covertly protecting Wakandan interests in the outside world. When Hunter's plans fall apart, the Dogs are reconstituted by Queen Shuri. Following the People's terrorist attacks, a reformed *Hatut Zeraze*—operating under strict guidelines—becomes an official arm of reinstated King T'Challa's military forces.

DATA FILE

FIRST APPEARANCE: *Black Panther* (Vol. 3) #4 (Feb. 1999)

OCCUPATION: Secret police force, paramilitary mercenaries, elite special ops soldiers

AIMS: Defense of Wakanda

AFFILIATIONS: Wakandan Royal Family, *Dora Milaje*, Wakandan Army

POWERS/ABILITIES: Vibranium-augmented uniforms; cutting-edge military weapons; advanced surveillance, stealth, and cloaking technologies

> *"The Zeraze knew **exactly** where to hit me."*
>
> IRON MAN

Hatut Zeraze problem-solving usually involves deadly force delivered by lethal artillery.

The Dogs are ready for action in any locale or environment.

Dogs of War

The *Hatut Zeraze* is a cadre of elite, ultra-patriotic Wakandan warriors and espionage specialists. Each recruit is trained in multiple combat specialities and surveillance protocols. All members are able to blend into any environment, and are deadly fighters in the air, on the ground, or underwater. They are strong, relentless, and wholly dedicated to their leader and Wakanda.

HATUT ZERAZE

Unknown and unloved, the *Hatut Zeraze* has watched over Wakanda for decades like a team of belligerent ghosts. Fanatically loyal to their leader, the Dogs of War are remorseless and always ready to give up their lives for their god and country.

THE HIDDEN KINGDOM

Situated by Lake Nyanza (Victoria) in East Africa, Wakanda is bordered by mountains to the north and west, and swamps to the south. The populace comprises 18 self-governing tribes, each electing representatives to a Council of Elders—Taifa Ngao —presided over by the ruling Black Panther. The country has six Birnins or metropolitan centres housing millions of citizens. Each Birnin specializes in one area of culture or industry, like the "city of knowledge," Birnin Azzaria, where science and education are paramount. Savagely repulsing every invasion for millennia, Wakanda has progressed in secure isolation and is now regarded as the most scientifically sophisticated civilization on Earth.

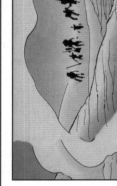

Wakanda

JABARI-LANDS

The mountainous Jabari-Lands have always been a hotbed of rebellion. The people worship the primal White Gorilla, and tribal leaders have often sought power and popularity by attempting to supplant Wakanda's dominant Panther Clan. Following the war against the superhuman terrorist cell the People, the region became a protectorate for women and families rescued from slavery by the Midnight Angels' "No One Man" movement.

REPUBLIC OF MOHANNDA

Ravaged by civil war, Mohannda was ruthlessly exploited by arms manufacturer Cardinal Technologies. The Republic's wilderness region contains the mystic volcanic phenomenon the Heart of Africa. Its hereditary shamans created the magically empowered warrior Afrikaa, who ended Cardinal's schemes with Black Panther's aid.

MOHANNDA

Birnin T'Chaka ◉

Birnin Djata ◉

WARRIOR FALLS

Located on the River of Grace and Wisdom between Mount Kanda and Mount Wakanda, Warrior Falls is a stunning natural arena for the ritual challenge for leadership of the Panther Clan and the nation.

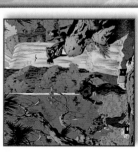

BIRNIN ZANA—THE GOLDEN CITY

The ruling Black Panther and Taifa Ngao meet in Wakanda's administrative capital Birnin Zana. The "Golden City" is the nation's showpiece, filled with gleaming towers and municipal marvels like monorails and floating sidewalks. The city boasts monumental Panther idols and is home to the Royal Palace, Golden City Polytechnic Prep, the Upanga training center for the *Dora Milaje*, and the Fort Hahn prison. Rising from the lake encircling Birnin Zana is the iconic City of the Dead, Necropolis, perpetually lit by a beacon of light.

Nyanza
(Lake Victoria)

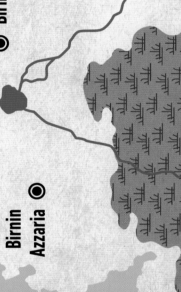

ALKAMA FIELDS

The south-eastern border region separating Wakanda from Niganda holds the Alkama Fields, vast fertile plains providing abundant crops and supporting a huge cattle industry. Considered the breadbasket of the nation, Alkama Fields is claimed by Niganda as its territory, illegally stolen by Wakanda in an ancient tribal feud.

WAKANDA

Warrior Falls

Mena Ngai
(The Great Mound)

Birnin
Bashenga ◉

● **Birnin S'Yan**

Birnin
Azzaria ◉

NIGANDA

REPUBLIC OF NIGANDA

Niganda is a rival nation that blames centuries of poverty and instability on losing the bountiful Alkama Fields to Wakanda in a bygone dispute. A series of dictators has led Niganda in attacks against Wakanda, leading to a state of perpetual conflict and constant exploitation by Western interests.

AZANIA

CANAAN

KINGDOM OF CANAAN

Failed state Canaan was conquered by arms dealer Moses Magnum as a proposed homeland for African-Americans. However, his program of industrial expansion was merely a ploy to attack Wakanda for its Vibranium. After Magnum's defeat by Black Panther and cyborg hero Deathlok, Canaan slumped into anarchy and disorder.

REPUBLIC OF AZANIA

A last bastion of white colonial rule in Africa, Azania is a highly militarized, apartheid-governed country. The state maintains a tenuous grip on power using advanced weaponry and its own patriotic superhuman defenders, known as the Supremacists.

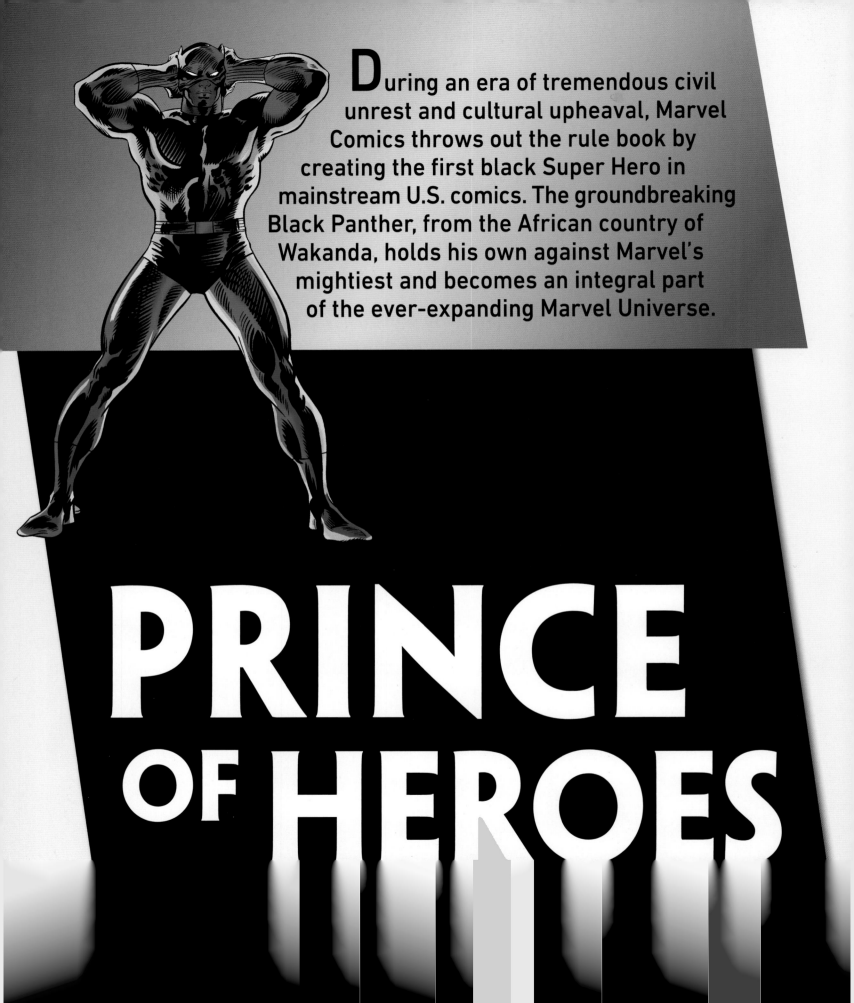

During an era of tremendous civil unrest and cultural upheaval, Marvel Comics throws out the rule book by creating the first black Super Hero in mainstream U.S. comics. The groundbreaking Black Panther, from the African country of Wakanda, holds his own against Marvel's mightiest and becomes an integral part of the ever-expanding Marvel Universe.

PRINCE OF HEROES

***Fantastic Four* (Vol. 1) #53 (Aug. 1966)**
T'Challa's tragic origin is revealed as the formidable
adversary is transformed into Marvel's newest star.

***Captain America* (Vol. 1) #100 (Apr. 1968)**
After battling alongside Captain America, T'Challa is
recommended for membership of the Avengers.

***The Avengers* (Vol. 1) #53 (Jun. 1968)**
The Black Panther's first Avengers mission brings
him into conflict with the X-Men and Magneto!

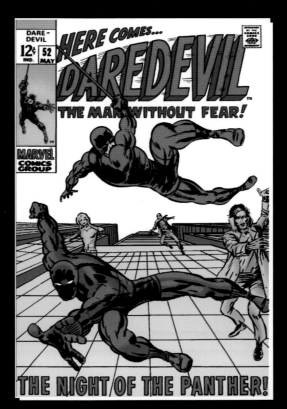

***Daredevil* (Vol. 1) #52 (May 1969)**
T'Challa meets the hero whom he will one day
replace as Hell's Kitchen's Man Without Fear.

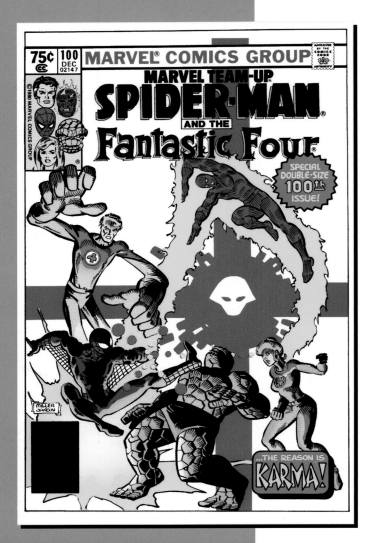

MARVEL TEAM-UP (VOL.1) #100

A FORGOTTEN CHILDHOOD FLAME IS REKINDLED WHEN A VENGEFUL ENEMY REAPPEARS.

Before T'Challa can become a king, he has to become a man. However, undertaking his people's traditional Rite of Passage almost ends in the prince becoming a hostage and slave of an enemy state. Happily, his initiation intersects with the path of a young mutant girl he will one day come to call my "White Lioness." Her name is Ororo Munroe.

DECEMBER 1980

MAIN CHARACTERS
Black Panther (T'Challa) • Storm (Ororo Munroe)

SUPPORTING CHARACTERS
Andreas de Ruyter • Unnamed assassin

MAIN LOCATIONS
New York City • Wakandan Embassy, Manhattan • Long Island • Ethiopia • Kenya

1 In New York City, a hidden assassin fails to murder Ororo Munroe, a.k.a. weather-manipulating mutant Storm. She easily subdues him and learns that the shooter was hired by Andreas de Ruyter to kill her and King T'Challa of Wakanda. On hearing these names, Ororo recalls how, at the age of 12, she had trekked across the African continent looking for a place to call home.

2 On that epic journey, Ororo helps a Wakandan youth named T'Challa as he is about to be abducted by South African soldiers led by political opportunist Andreas "the Bull" de Ruyter.

3 The youngsters then spend precious weeks together before the prince's sense of duty and Storm's own restlessness force them apart. Now, after several years, their old foe de Ruyter has returned, and Ororo rushes to warn her childhood sweetheart that his life is in danger once again.

4 A joyful reunion at the Wakandan Embassy rekindles old feelings for both heroes. However, happiness turns to grim determination once T'Challa's information-gathering resources track down their nemesis to Long Island. Infiltrating de Ruyter's heavily fortified mansion, they find the place suspiciously easy to enter.

"For years I planned my revenge... and once I found your woman, I set my plan in motion!"

ANDREAS DE RUYTER

5 Working together, Storm and the Black Panther hunt their enemy until confronted by a deadly giant robot mind-linked to de Ruyter. The heroic duo soon get the upper hand in the battle, and the shock of his mechanical minion's destruction creates a psychic feedback that kills the Bull.

6 With the vengeful madman dispatched, Ororo and T'Challa part once again. Both are filled with regret over missed opportunities, but also a wary anticipation of what may lie ahead.

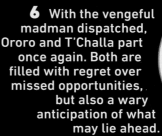

THE STUDENT PRINCE

As a youth, T'Challa's extensive education takes him to many prestigious colleges, but it is in the U.S. that his path in life is firmly established. He finds love, encounters prejudice, and loses his greatest friend.

> *"Devils and wolves and ghosts. Why stop now?"*
>
> NIKKI ADAMS

NIKKI ADAMS

Nicole Adams is an outspoken student taking the same classes at the U.S. college T'Challa attends after he graduates from Oxford University in Britain. They fall in love, but the affair provokes hostile reactions from fellow students. When Nikki learns that "Luke Charles" is an alias masking T'Challa's regal status, the prince's bodyguard, Zuri, ensures that the pair split up.

Years later, following a glittering career in the U.S. State Department, Nikki briefly reconnects with T'Challa after assigning her fiancé, Everett K. Ross, to be his U.S. liaison. She is later kidnapped and taken to Wakanda, before being killed by Black Panther foe, Malice.

N'BAZA

Despite declaring himself just a simple witch doctor, N'Baza is a trusted advisor of King T'Chaka and regarded as an unofficial uncle by the Royal Family. After Queen Ramonda's disappearance and T'Chaka's murder, Orphan Prince T'Challa comes to rely on N'Baza's wisdom.

N'Baza rules as co-regent beside S'Yan, who—as T'Chaka's brother—becomes the next Black Panther. N'Baza supervises T'Challa's education, sending him to Europe and the U.S., and dispatching his own son B'Tumba to be the prince's companion. N'Baza's death results in T'Challa's first leave of absence from the Avengers.

B'TUMBA

B'Tumba grows up with the children of the Royal Family and becomes T'Challa's closest childhood friend. As such, B'Tumba is his father N'Baza's only choice to accompany the young prince when he ventures into the wider world to study.

Yet amid the temptations and glamor of the West, B'Tumba grows jealous of his friend's easy successes in both academic and sporting arenas. Seizing on his resentment, B'Tumba is recruited by A.I.M. with promises of wealth and power, and he is used to spearhead a secret expedition into Wakanda to steal Vibranium. At the critical moment, however, B'Tumba refuses to kill T'Challa, sacrificing himself instead.

ZURI

Considered Wakanda's mightiest warrior, Zuri is a comrade and companion of T'Chaka. After the king's death, the loyal veteran becomes T'Challa's bodyguard and mentor during the prince's overseas education, ensuring he remains true to his country's values. Brusque and patriotic, Zuri proves to be a valued confidant during T'Challa's reign, even grudgingly accepting some outworlders, such as Thor and Monica Rambeau, as worthy allies. Zuri dies valiantly alongside W'Kabi, defending the wounded T'Challa from the totem-devourer, Morlun.

KAMAL RAKIM

College student Kamal Rakim is a passionate civil rights activist who sometimes resorts to violence to further his cause. One day, he and a gang of like-minded radicals attack fellow student Luke Charles—in reality Prince T'Challa—for dating white woman Nikki Adams. The assault and a confrontation with royal bodyguard Zuri results in the lovers separating.

After graduating, Rakim translates his ideals into a successful political career. Years later, while serving as a U.S. senator, he meets T'Challa at a state function for the visiting king of Wakanda. The two resolve their differences and Rakim urges the Black Panther to use his position and reputation to become a symbol for all African-Americans.

AVENGERS ASSEMBLED

After battling alongside the Fantastic Four, the Inhumans, and Captain America, T'Challa realizes that a growing tide of superhuman menaces is proliferating beyond Wakanda's borders. To study these potential threats or possible allies, the Black Panther happily accepts Captain America's offer to take his place in the mighty Avengers.

The Avengers (Vol. 1) #52 (May 1968)
Although confident he can overpower his captors, the Black Panther decides to play a waiting game.

The Avengers (Vol. 1) #52 (May 1968)
The Avengers' security devices are no match for the Black Panther's incredible agility and ingenuity.

STRANGER IN TOWN

Landing in New York City, the Black Panther heads straight for Avengers Mansion. Instead of a welcoming reception, he finds the Avengers' headquarters in darkness and that the security codes given to him by Captain America do not work. Fearing the worst, T'Challa breaks in, quickly defeating the building's many automatic defenses. He works his way to the team's nerve center where he encounters a shocking scene: three dead Avengers!

IN THE HEAT OF THE NIGHT

Goliath, Hawkeye, and the Wasp lie cold and motionless on the floor, but before the Panther can investigate further, he is arrested by visiting S.H.I.E.L.D. agent Jasper Sitwell. Assuming the cat-like stranger to be the Avengers' murderer, Sitwell summons the police who unmask T'Challa and take him into custody. Their quiet, patient prisoner prefers to gather all the facts before taking action.

DON'T FEAR THE REAPER

Deducing that his arrival was anticipated by some enemy determined to frame him, the Black Panther escapes and races back to Avengers Mansion. He finds the Grim Reaper hiding at the scene of the crime and attacks. In the heat of battle, the gloating villain reveals that the Avengers are not dead...yet. Before T'Challa first arrived, the mysterious maniac had used his electronic scythe to plunge them all into a deathlike coma.

> ## "T'Challa, son of T'Chaka... welcome to the Avengers!"
> GOLIATH

The Avengers (Vol. 1) #52 (May 1968) *Defying police gunfire, the Panther uses an electrical charge to neutralize the effects of the Reaper's scythe and revive the dying Avengers.*

The Avengers (Vol. 1) #55 (Aug. 1968) *From the outset the Black Panther was at the vanguard of every Avengers mission.*

DYING HOURS

Learning that the condition afflicting the Avengers will become permanent within hours, T'Challa defeats the Reaper and leaves him apparently dying. Despite being wounded by the Reaper's scythe, the Black Panther rushes to the hospital and tears his way through an army of outraged lawmen to revive the heroes just in time. However, when they all return to Avengers Mansion, the Grim Reaper has vanished.

TEAM PLAYER

With the immediate danger over, the resurrected Avengers welcome the Wakandan king into their hallowed ranks and begin clearing him for duty. Having seen the valor of his new comrades, T'Challa prepares for a great change in his life, temporarily at least. Appointing regents to govern Wakanda in his absence, the Black Panther opts to serve a greater kingdom—the whole of mankind itself!

The Avengers (Vol. 1) #52 (May 1968) *The savage struggle sees speed and agility pitted against super-science and the strength of madness.*

The Avengers (Vol. 1) #52 (May 1968) *The Avengers' heartfelt welcome to the team moved T'Challa far more than he expected.*

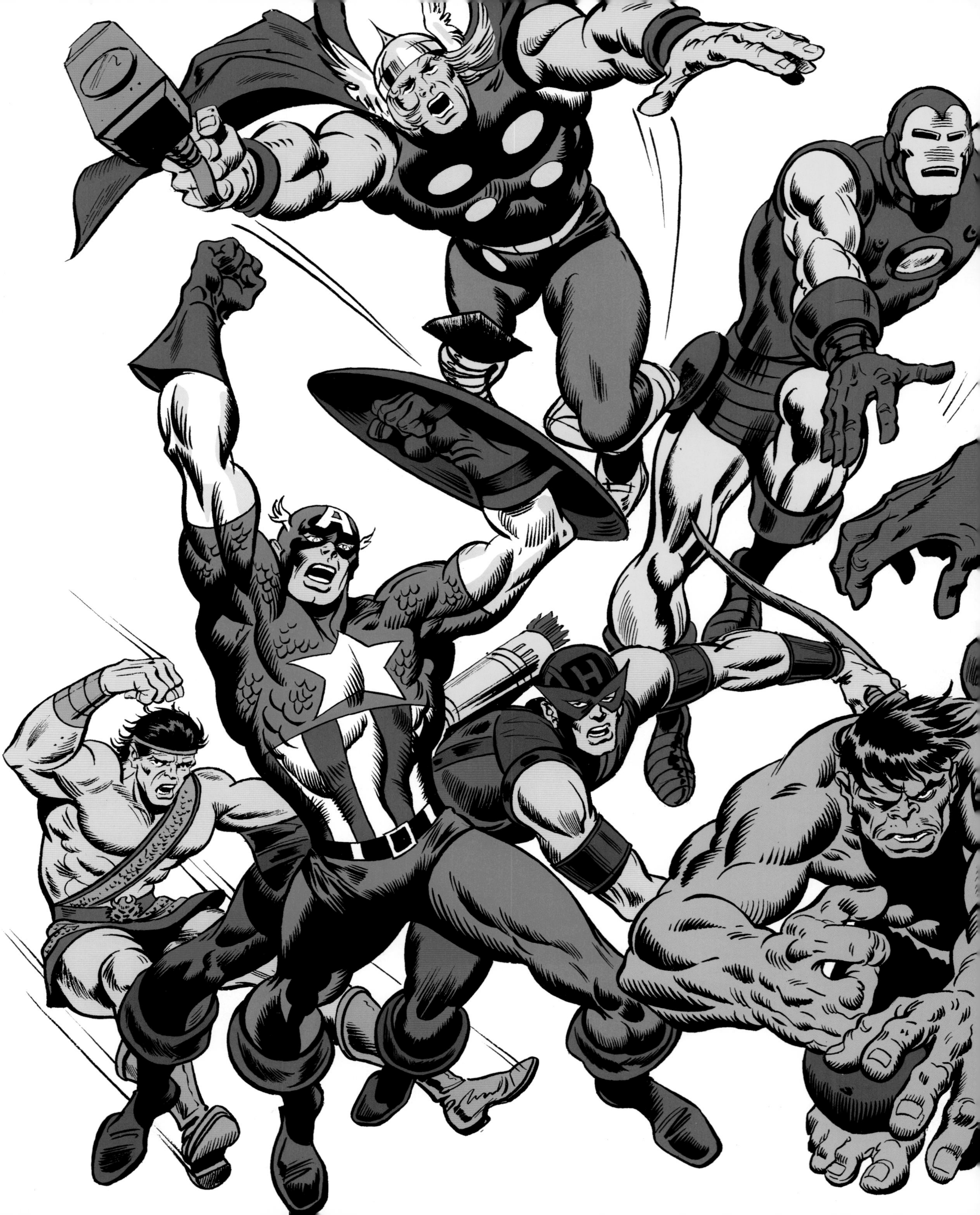

The Avengers Annual (Vol. 1) #2 (Sep. 1968)
Superteams are all about action and spectacle. This panoramic pin-up set readers' pulses racing by celebrating the Black Panther joining the most powerful pantheon of costumed crusaders ever assembled.

A.I.M.

Once Wakanda lost its cloak of international anonymity, the country's incredible riches, resources, and advanced technology made it a certain target for plunderers. One organization always out to gain advantage by pillaging from others is A.I.M., an unscrupulous, radical collective of hi-tech raiders.

Big ideas

Despite constantly subdividing into warring factions, A.I.M.'s fanatical commitment to forced global change has lethal and sometimes universe-threatening consequences. Among its most catastrophic creations are artificially mutated psionic assassins such as M.O.D.O.K. (Mental Organism Designed Only for Killing), power-mimicking Super-Adaptoids, deadly super-plagues, and reality-reshaping Cosmic Cubes. Moreover, what A.I.M. cannot invent it tries to steal—everything from Iron Man's armor to rare natural resources like Vibranium.

> *"A.I.M.'s mission is going well... efficiency and surprise have subdued all opposition!"*
>
> A.I.M. SCIENTIST

ORIGIN

Advanced Idea Mechanics begins during World War II, as a scientific think tank convened by Nazi officer Baron Wolfgang von Strucker to gain political and economic power through technological intervention. Governed by a succession of Supreme Scientists, A.I.M. pursues conquest while selling its inventions and weapons to other clandestine groups and rogue governments.

With Wakandan Vibranium strictly controlled, A.I.M. repeatedly targets the mineral from the country's Sacred Mound, using every tactic from bribery and subversion to outright theft. However, every attempt is thwarted by the vigilance and power of the Black Panther. When A.I.M. turns its attention to securing Savage Land Vibranium, Black Panther Shuri, Ka-Zar, Shanna the She-Devil, and S.H.I.E.L.D. stand in its way.

DATA FILE

REAL NAME: Advanced Idea Mechanics

FIRST APPEARANCE: *Strange Tales* (Vol. 1) #146 (Jul. 1966)

MISSION STATEMENT: Replacement of the world order by radical technological innovation

AFFILIATIONS: Hydra, Intelligencia, T.H.E.M.

BASE: A.I.M. Island; Boca Caliente; various hidden bases

ZEMO IMPOSTOR

When Nazi scientist Baron Zemo dies battling Captain America, his pilot assumes the villain's identity and plunders his various discoveries. Over a number of years, he hires mercenaries and equips a hidden African base on the border of Wakanda. Eventually, the fraud's efforts bear fruit and he activates Zemo's greatest weapon—an orbiting solar death-ray—with the intention of holding the world to ransom. When test firings endanger Wakanda, T'Challa invites Captain America to join him and together they wreck the scheme and destroy the terror weapon. The impostor is eventually killed by his own outraged troops.

ANDREAS DE RUYTER

Proud, rich, and privileged Andreas de Ruyter is a powerful and influential figure in South Africa who plans to seize young T'Challa as the boy undergoes his ritual walkabout. His scheme to control the future king fails due to the intervention of teenaged mutant Ororo Munroe, who has befriended the Prince on his trek. After the pair escape, a humiliated de Ruyter spends decades and a small fortune engineering a fitting revenge. However, when that opportunity finally arises, the villain perishes after using hired assassins and a giant robot in a failed attempt to eliminate the adult Storm and Black Panther.

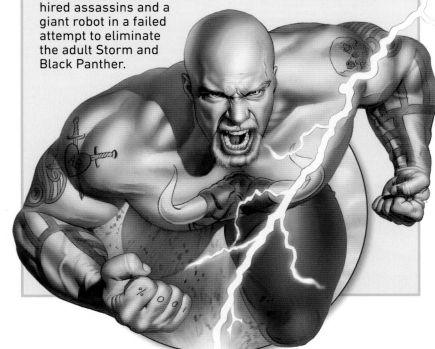

MARAUDERS

Despite its advanced culture and strict isolation, Wakanda and its Orphan Prince never lack for ambitious enemies. Whether seeking conquest, political advantage, or the miraculous mineral Vibranium, greedy interlopers always underestimate the Black Panther's power and resolve.

PSYCHO-MAN

From the subatomic microverse, the alien Psycho-Man uses giant robotic bodies to operate in the greater universe. His weapons are advanced technologies that create illusions and manipulate emotions to dominate minds and warp personalities. Originally seeking new colony worlds for his overpopulated homeworld, the vain, vindictive Psycho-Man grows obsessed with the Black Panther and Fantastic Four, who continually foil his schemes.

PRECIOUS METAL

A colossal meteor crashes into prehistoric Wakanda, forever altering the country's destiny. The ore is mined to enhance weapons and brings great wealth. However, it also makes monsters of many men, leading to the birth of the ferociously protective Panther Cult.

HERE BE MONSTERS

Vibranium radiation permeates Wakanda and is probably responsible for the power-enhancing effects of the heart-shaped herb and unique beasts, such as the carnivorous highland White Gorillas. T'Challa's own half-brother, Jakarra, deliberately mutates himself with raw ore to gain overwhelming power, before being destroyed by the Black Panther and his royal cousins.

Black Panther (Vol. 1) #10 (Jul. 1978)

UNNATURAL RESOURCES

For centuries, processed Vibranium has been sold in minute and strictly regulated quantities, making Wakanda one of Earth's richest nations. As physics and engineering in the outside world catch up to Wakandan levels, the metal—a secret element in Captain America's indestructible shield—is increasingly sought by corrupt corporations, enemy nations, and clandestine criminal organizations such as Latveria, Roxxon, and Advanced Idea Mechanics.

Doomwar (Vol. 1) #1 (Apr. 2010)

MAGICAL MINERAL

Early in Wakandan history, shamans discover Vibranium's most terrifying characteristic: the mineral can be used to amplify and augment magic and sorcery. This knowledge is suppressed, with only the Black Panthers and the priesthood remaining party to the secret over successive centuries.

Doomwar (Vol. 1) #1 (Apr. 2010)

SHOCK AND ORE

Vibranium is an extraterrestrial element that exists in two forms. The isotope beneath the Antarctic Savage Land is a variant that destroys metals, while the primary property of the meteor that falls in Wakanda is to absorb all vibration, from sound waves to kinetic shock.

Wakanda's Great Mound of raw Vibranium proves to be both boon and menace to the country. Emitting low levels of a mysterious radiation, sustained exposure to the unprocessed ore in its unprocessed state can cause mutation in extra-susceptible organisms. Many mutated monsters are created before Wakanda's Black Panther Cult finally harnesses the mineral's miraculous, nation-building properties.

Black Panther (Vol. 1) #7 (Jan. 1978)

When not ruling Wakanda from afar or fighting evil as an Avenger, T'Challa becomes involved in African-American issues in his civilian guise as schoolteacher "Luke Charles". However, the growing demands on him as a Super Hero soon take precedence.

MAN OF MYSTERY

***Fantastic Four Annual* (Vol. 1) #5 (Nov. 1967)**
An invasion from the microverse finds T'Challa and
the Inhumans facing Psycho-Man on Panther Island.

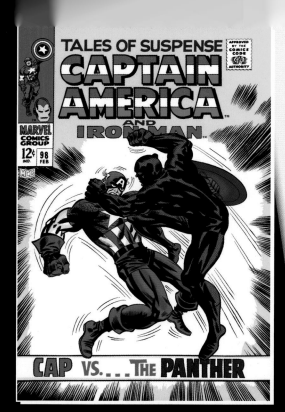

***Tales of Suspense* (Vol. 1) #98 (Feb. 1968)**
T'Challa tests Captain America's mettle, before the two
heroes unite to tackle a resurrected Baron Zemo.

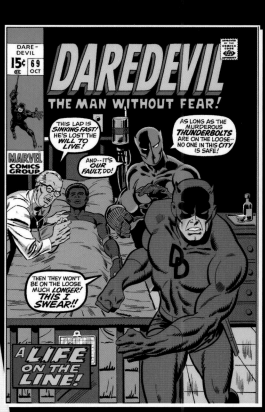

***Daredevil* (Vol. 1) #69 (Oct. 1970)**
Daredevil and the Panther join forces against a
street gang corrupting high school students.

***Fantastic Four* (Vol. 1) #119 (Feb. 1972)**
The Fantastic Four comes to the rescue when the "Black
Leopard" is imprisoned in apartheid-ruled Rudyarda.

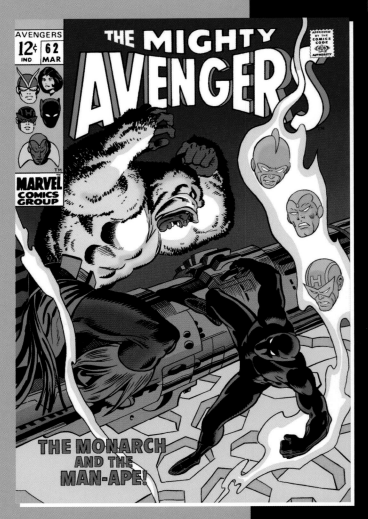

THE AVENGERS (VOL. 1) #62

THE BLACK PANTHER RETURNS TO WAKANDA AND DISCOVERS A THREAT TO HIS RULE.

After saving Earth from destruction by the fire demon Surtur and the ice giant Ymir, the Black Panther invites his Avenger allies to visit Wakanda. It is the king's first visit home since leaving Africa, but he is confident that his trusted regent, M'Baku, has ruled wisely in his absence...

MARCH 1969

MAIN CHARACTERS

T'Challa • Avengers (Vision, Hawkeye) • Black Knight • M'Baku the Man-Ape

SUPPORTING CHARACTERS

W'Kabi • N'Gamo

MAIN LOCATIONS

Techno Organic Jungle • Royal Palace Compound • Wakanda's atomic furnace

1 As the Avengers disembark from T'Challa's personal aircraft, they are attacked by murderous Wakandan soldiers. After T'Challa ends the assault, M'Baku and his scheming lackey N'Gamo claim the incident is a stupid misunderstanding brought on by the guards' over-zealousness.

2 In reality, M'Baku has secretly embraced the forbidden White Gorilla Cult. With newly gained super-strength, he plans to defeat T'Challa in hand-to-hand combat and claim the throne. The schemer's first move is to get rid of the Avengers by drugging them at a welcome banquet held in their honor.

"...A new day had dawned in Wakanda...the day of the Man-Ape!"

M'BAKU

3 With his subjects observing the challenge, the Panther engages the Man-Ape in battle. The brutal struggle rages across the Royal Compound and into the atomic furnace facility deep beneath Wakanda.

4 On the brink of victory, T'Challa attempts to save his beaten challenger from the radioactive flames, but is repaid with treachery.

5 The Black Panther awakens strapped to a marble altar. The maddened Man-Ape boasts that T'Challa's death will signal an end to technological advancement and a return to darkness and primeval savagery in Wakanda.

6 When the exultant Man-Ape attempts to bury the drugged T'Challa beneath his own sacred panther totem, it crumbles. The colossal statue crushes the would-be usurper, burying his crazed dreams of great power.

M'BAKU
THE MAN-APE

M'Baku wants his savage religion to eclipse all others and his people to dominate the tribal federation of Wakanda. He betrays friends, slaughters enemies, brings his people to the edge of extinction, and finally gives his life to his maniacal cause.

ORIGIN

When T'Challa joins the Avengers, the Wakandan monarch appoints M'Baku as regent, but his deputy craves more. The Jabari tribal chieftain chooses to secretly worship an outlawed cult, and mystically gains immense strength and virtual invulnerability by killing a white gorilla, bathing in its blood, and eating its flesh. M'Baku wants to banish all the technological advances of the forward-looking Panther Cult, returning Wakanda to an era of primal brutality where strength and ruthlessness prevail.

Disgraced when T'Challa wins their ritual duel, M'Baku becomes a super-powered mercenary, transferring his hatred to all Avengers and joining many villainous groups intent on destroying Earth's Mightiest Heroes.

Man-Ape wears tribal adornments made from teeth and bone.

M'Baku maintains a connection to his god by wearing the pelt of the white gorilla he has killed.

Faithful unto death

Suffering humiliating defeats, M'Baku returns to his homeland, promoting his beliefs within Jabari's borders. His people have been sidelined long before his attempted coup and the Man-Ape offers hope to his broken followers.

The Jabari are decimated when the Devourer-of-Totems, Morlun, crosses their country to consume T'Challa's Panther Spirit. Undaunted, M'Baku charges the immortal predator and dies, defiant to the last.

DATA FILE

REAL NAME: M'Baku

FIRST APPEARANCE: *The Mighty Avengers* (Vol. 1) #62 (Mar. 1969)

OCCUPATION: Leader of Jabari tribe, revolutionary, mercenary

AFFILIATIONS: Jabari Tribe, White Gorilla Cult, Lethal Legion, Masters of Evil, Villains for Hire

POWERS/ABILITIES: Mystically enhanced strength, agility, reflexes, and durability

BASE: Jabari village, Wakanda

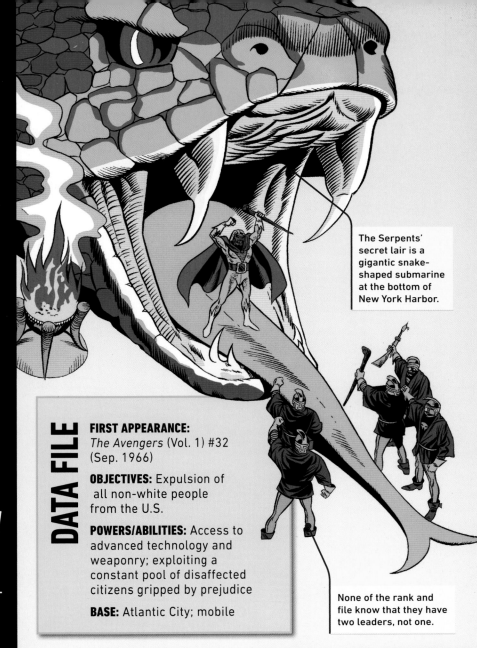

The Serpents' secret lair is a gigantic snake-shaped submarine at the bottom of New York Harbor.

None of the rank and file know that they have two leaders, not one.

ORIGIN

The Sons of the Serpent incite racial hatred, perpetrating acts of brutality against ethnic minorities. The group's goal is to remove the "foreign-born and unfit" from U.S. soil. Although the Serpents' leaders change, its ranks are filled by ordinary citizens driven by prejudice and discontent.

The Sons of the Serpent's first incarnation is established by foreign warlord General Chen who—until exposed by the Avengers—provides resources and strategies to turn U.S. citizens against each other. Later versions of the organization include a team assembled by a financier to increase his personal fortune, a cabal that worshiped the corrupt Elder God, Set, and a well-placed conspiracy of policemen, lawyers, and judges who abuse the law to target innocent foreigners.

> "As the first serpent drove Adam and Eve from Eden... so shall we **drive from this land the foreign-born...the inferior!**"
>
> SONS OF THE SERPENT

DATA FILE

FIRST APPEARANCE:
The Avengers (Vol. 1) #32 (Sep. 1966)

OBJECTIVES: Expulsion of all non-white people from the U.S.

POWERS/ABILITIES: Access to advanced technology and weaponry; exploiting a constant pool of disaffected citizens gripped by prejudice

BASE: Atlantic City; mobile

Cat among the serpents
White celebrity Dan Dunn and black activist Montague Hale form a group targeting African-Americans. Alternating as the Supreme Serpent, they inflame viewers with hate-speech, bombings, and beatings, but fail when their assault on singer Monica Lynne brings them into conflict with the Black Panther. Although captured and framed, T'Challa's skills and Monica's bravery ensure the Sons of the Serpent are brought to justice.

SONS OF THE SERPENT

Racial and social divisions never die and many opportunistic power-seekers exploit prejudice to further their own agendas. Through the Sons of the Serpent, unscrupulous masterminds have converted the bigoted and prejudiced into a terrifying paramilitary force for personal gain.

SERPENTS IN PARADISE

Across the U.S., racial tensions mount, stoked by rival New York TV pundits Dan Dunn and Montague Hale. Into this tinderbox, the white supremacist group Sons of the Serpent reappear, attacking African-Americans and fueling the fire. Worse still, the police—and even the Avengers—seem helpless to catch the masked bigots.

The Avengers (Vol. 1) #73 (Feb. 1970)
Enraged at their brutal racism, the Black Panther single-handedly takes on the Serpents.

TRIAL BY TELEVISION

Returning to New York after visiting Wakanda, the Black Panther discovers the city is on the brink of a race riot. On his way to Avengers Mansion, he saves performer Monica Lynne who is about to be abducted by Serpent soldiers following her televised appearance on the *Dan Dunn Show*.

The Avengers (Vol. 1) #73 (Feb. 1970)
Black Panther leaps into action against three Serpents as they attempt to kidnap singer Monica Lynne.

CAT FIGHT

Reunited with his Avengers comrades, T'Challa is incensed by the actions of the Sons of the Serpents and the inflammatory speeches of the television stars, who seem determined to incite further violence. He demands to be allowed to tackle the Serpents alone, and is granted 24 hours to catch them.

> "The **Black Panther** knows well the scent of evil!"
>
> **BLACK PANTHER**

The Avengers (Vol. 1) #74 (Mar. 1970) The assembled Avengers' Panther hunt ends when they are ambushed by the Serpents' aircraft.

The Avengers (Vol. 1) #73 (Feb. 1970) Despite all his stealth and guile, the Panther is captured by the Serpents on their submarine.

SNAKE HUNT

Tirelessly prowling the night, T'Challa tracks his prey to the docks and overpowers one of the masked thugs. Dressed in the villain's robes, he joins a squad of Serpents returning to a huge snake-like submarine hidden in the depths off Manhattan Island. However, he is exposed when he cannot recite the Serpent oath of allegiance.

The Avengers (Vol. 1) #74 (Mar. 1970) The Supreme Serpent exhorts his fanatical followers to greater acts of intimidation.

AGAINST THE AVENGERS

When the Black Panther suddenly begins to attack businesses supporting the Serpents, the Avengers attempt to stop him. The clash ends in disaster after a skycraft captures the Panther and escapes. With Monica's help, the Avengers locate a TV studio where the Serpents are promising to unmask T'Challa as a criminal anarchist live on air.

The Avengers (Vol. 1) #74 (Mar. 1970) T'Challa's on-air revelation enables the real Black Panther to expose and shatter Dunn and Hale's scheme.

THE AWFUL TRUTH

Escaping imprisonment, T'Challa finally exposes the anarchist Panther as a Serpent impostor on live television. Yellowjacket and the Wasp similarly unmask the Supreme Serpent as being both Dunn and Hale, who have taken turns to play the villain. The rival TV presenters are revealed as greedy demagogues keen to create a crisis and manipulate hotheads on both sides to gain power for themselves.

A KING'S COMRADES

During his service with the Avengers in the U.S., T'Challa encounters numerous Super Heroes. He battles alongside most—and even against some— but eventually all emerge as valued allies, with a few becoming trusted confidants of the hero-king.

SPIDER-MAN

Young, idealistic, and driven by guilt, Peter Parker uses powers derived from a mutated spider bite to save lives as Spider-Man. Black Panther's first experience of the wondrous Wall-Crawler comes while saving him from Stegron the Dinosaur Man. As they defeat their foe together, T'Challa realizes the brash youngster's bravado conceals a deeply compassionate fellow scientist and a hero haunted by tragedy.

RED WOLF

Native-American William Talltrees helps the Avengers defeat Zodiac boss Cornelius van Lunt. Although their interaction is limited, T'Challa soon realizes Red Wolf has abilities similar to his own, bestowed by Native American deity Owayodata, just as Black Panther's stem from African Panther God, Bast.

DOCTOR STRANGE

A former surgeon who finds new purpose through the study of magic, Stephen Strange defends humanity from ancient, arcane terrors and modern nightmares. Soon after meeting T'Challa at the wedding of Yellowjacket and the Wasp, Strange seeks the Avengers' aid to defeat ice giant Ymir and save Wakanda and the world from fire-demon Surtur. He later becomes a key ally in T'Challa's Illuminati group.

BLACK WIDOW

Russian superspy Natasha Romanoff, a.k.a. the Black Widow, first encounters T'Challa when the Grim Reaper frames him for murdering the Avengers. Before long, she is fighting beside the Panther— initially against Egghead, Puppet Master, and the Mad Thinker as the villains try to blackmail the world—and ultimately as a fully fledged fellow Avenger.

CAPTAIN MARVEL (MAR-VELL)

A Kree warrior sent to spy on humanity, Mar-Vell eventually defects. Becoming Protector of the Universe, he founds a dynasty of galactic heroes before dying from cancer. The cosmic champion first encounters T'Challa when the Mad Titan Thanos attacks Earth as part of a diabolical scheme to secure the Cosmic Cube and become a god.

BROTHER VOODOO/ DOCTOR VOODOO

Sharing his body with his murdered brother Daniel, psychologist Jericho Drumm uses the sorcerous arts of Voodoo to battle oppression and mystic menaces. Drumm first works with T'Challa when Black Panther and Ben Grimm (Thing) battle a Vampire Zuvembie who has been abducting prominent black people for African Super Villain Kinji Obatu.

HULK

Hulk is an unstoppable force of sheer fury, created when physicist Bruce Banner is caught in the blast of his own gamma bomb. When the Hulk is trapped underground and rampaging towards the San Andreas Fault, the Avengers are called in to stop him. T'Challa uses a Gammatron Bombarder to divert and drive off the brute. Sometime later, when Banner has regained some control over his bestial form, he briefly joins the Illuminati to help avert a cosmic cataclysm.

CULTURE

Nurtured by divine Bast, Wakandan history begins at the dawn of civilization. A rich and complex culture developed, with Wakandans cherishing technological progress as much as arcane traditions. Blessed with fertile soil and Vibranium, Wakanda's people have flourished as they have never sought to over-exploit the country's vast natural resources.

OUT OF BALANCE

Proudly rationalist and forward thinking, Western-educated T'Challa ascends the throne and bans sorcery, exiling self-serving magicians like Zawavari. Although mystic practices vanish from the cities, they thrive in remote regions. Many Wakandans, including Queen Mother Ramonda, still consult "witch-men," and eventually national emergencies force T'Challa to rescind his anti-magic laws.

Black Panther (Vol. 5) #3 (Jun. 2009)

KIMOYO CONNECTIVITY

From birth all Wakandans join the Kimoyo ("of the Spirit") Intranet system, a Vibranium-based supercomputer network. Accessed by cards or electronic beads, free universal services include holographic links to the national database, and telecommunications and entertainment services. Kimoyo beads also connect to Wakanda's healthcare system, and can ensure that if the nation is threatened, a call to arms reaches every potential defender.

Black Panther (Vol. 6) #13 (May 2017)

TIME-HONORED SOLUTIONS

The heart-shaped herb empowering Black Panthers is prepared by herbalists in strict accordance with ancient religious rites. Even after King T'Challa outlaws sorcery, the complex sacred ceremonies continue. Scientific research proves the herb is toxic to anyone not of royal blood, but no-one disputes that its ritual application grants feline attributes and allows a connection to Bast.

Black Panther: Panther's Prey (Vol. 1) #2 (Nov. 1990)

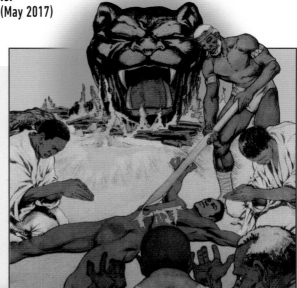

YESTERDAYS AND TOMORROWS

Wakanda embraces innovation and tradition without experiencing culture clash. Its Birnins are the most advanced cities on Earth, but many people prefer rural life, attuned to ancestral spirituality. For every Birnin Zana technician, numerous farmers and artisans thrive in suburban regions, employing technology only as necessary. For every city doctor, as many country shamans treat the sick with age-old cures. Wakandan students are fortunate enough to employ the most sophisticated learning tools on Earth to ensure they secure the best possible education.

Secret Wars (Vol. 1) #9 (Mar. 2016)

Safely established as a world-saving Avenger, the Black Panther wins his own solo comic series. The hero from Wakanda goes on to prove that contentious issues such as politics, religion, and revolution—combined with all-out action, adventure, and romance—always have a place in Marvel's universe.

DEFENDER OF THE FAITH

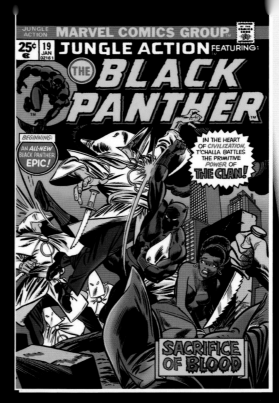

Jungle Action (Vol. 2) #14 (Mar. 1975)
T'Challa enters a primeval land hunting a foe hungry
to destroy everything the Wakandans believe in.

Jungle Action (Vol. 2) #19 (Jan. 1976)
Confronting America's racist past and present,
Black Panther begins his most challenging mission.

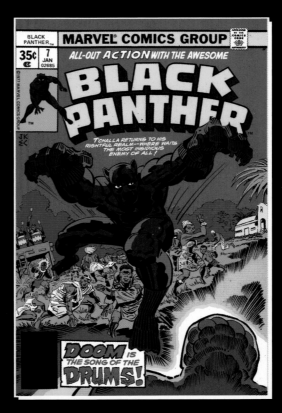

Daredevil Annual (Vol. 1) #4 (Oct. 1976)
T'Challa, Daredevil, and the Sub-Mariner clash
while averting disaster at a tidal power plant.

Black Panther (Vol. 1) #7 (Jan. 1978)
T'Challa reveals the secret origin of Wakanda's sacred
Panther Cult and its role in guarding Vibranium.

PANTHER'S RAGE

After too long abroad with the Avengers, T'Challa returns to Wakanda to quell a rebellion. He battles ruthless villains led by an unstoppable opponent, Killmonger, who is determined to tear down everything Black Panther stands for.

CRY, THE BELOVED COUNTRY

Returning to Wakanda and visiting the rural outlands, Black Panther discovers armed men torturing a farmer. Despite driving them off, T'Challa is too late to save his loyal subject. The man dies in his arms, thanking his adored chieftain for returning to his people at long last. As atrocities mount across Wakanda, the Panther's rage grows.

"We will take that place by force...and make it ours!"

KILLMONGER

Jungle Action (Vol. 2) #6 (Sep. 1973) *T'Challa is incensed when he spies an innocent farmer being tormented by Killmonger's men.*

TAKING THE OFFENSIVE

Surviving the plunge and nursed back to health by Monica Lynne, Black Panther is attacked by a succession of Killmonger's super-powered recruits. In retaliation, T'Challa and his most loyal Wakandan aides, Taku and W'Kabi, lead a military raid on the rebels' base—a seemingly ordinary rural village. The short, savage battle results in many captives for T'Challa and his allies.

RETURN OF THE NATIVE

While inspecting another massacred village, Black Panther finally confronts his elusive and murderous nemesis at Warrior Falls. Killmonger is someone T'Challa recently brought back to Wakanda from exile in the U.S. For all his power, the king is helpless before his foe's raw savagery, and is hurled to his imminent death in the roaring waters far below.

Jungle Action (Vol. 2) #6 (Sep. 1973) *Thrown by rebel leader Killmonger, Black Panther plunges into the churning waters.*

Jungle Action (Vol. 2) #11 (Sep. 1974) *During the battle, one of Killmonger's minions—Malice—appears and takes aim with her trident.*

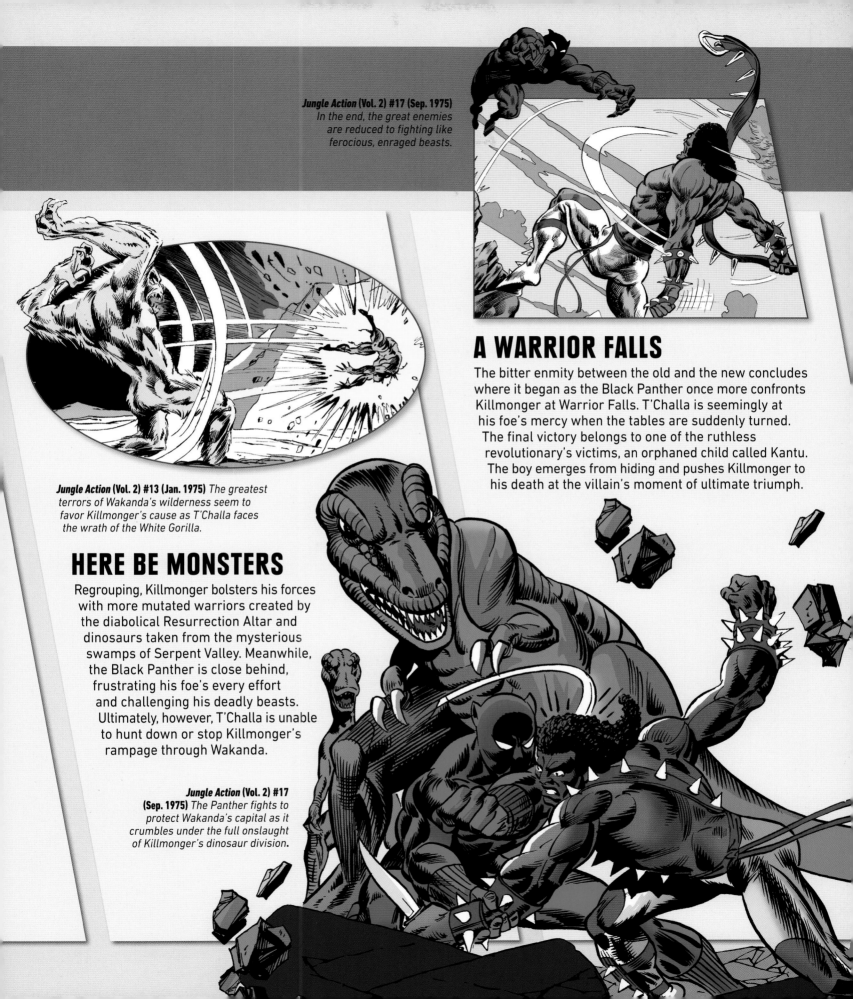

Jungle Action (Vol. 2) #17 (Sep. 1975)
In the end, the great enemies are reduced to fighting like ferocious, enraged beasts.

A WARRIOR FALLS

The bitter enmity between the old and the new concludes where it began as the Black Panther once more confronts Killmonger at Warrior Falls. T'Challa is seemingly at his foe's mercy when the tables are suddenly turned. The final victory belongs to one of the ruthless revolutionary's victims, an orphaned child called Kantu. The boy emerges from hiding and pushes Killmonger to his death at the villain's moment of ultimate triumph.

Jungle Action (Vol. 2) #13 (Jan. 1975) *The greatest terrors of Wakanda's wilderness seem to favor Killmonger's cause as T'Challa faces the wrath of the White Gorilla.*

HERE BE MONSTERS

Regrouping, Killmonger bolsters his forces with more mutated warriors created by the diabolical Resurrection Altar and dinosaurs taken from the mysterious swamps of Serpent Valley. Meanwhile, the Black Panther is close behind, frustrating his foe's every effort and challenging his deadly beasts. Ultimately, however, T'Challa is unable to hunt down or stop Killmonger's rampage through Wakanda.

Jungle Action (Vol. 2) #17 (Sep. 1975) *The Panther fights to protect Wakanda's capital as it crumbles under the full onslaught of Killmonger's dinosaur division.*

DEVIL'S DISCIPLES

Determined to seize and punish Wakanda, the villainous Erik Killmonger shows his contempt for king and country by launching an offensive on two fronts. While waging all-out war on his former homeland, he also sends a number of his deadly deputies against the Black Panther to weaken the monarch's resolve and spread terror throughout the African nation.

MALICE

Enhanced by Killmonger's science, Malice uses her extensive martial arts training, peak physical condition, and technologically advanced weaponry to bring destruction to Wakanda's Royal Palace. Her triple-bladed war spear can shear through stone or steel as if they were paper. Despite these advantages, she is eventually apprehended by Wakandan forces.

VENOMM

Disfigured by acid as a boy, Horatio Walters becomes a recluse, devoting his life to studying snakes. When Killmonger offers him a fresh start in Wakanda, Walters adopts the name Venomm and puts his knowledge of snakes and poisons to use as a deadly assassin. Captured by Wakandan forces and befriended by his jailer, Taku, Walters switches allegiance to the Black Panther's cause.

BARON MACABRE

Following his voluntary mutation on the Resurrection Altar, Baron Macabre can raise the dead and turn living victims into undead slaves. He reinforces these dark abilities with stolen Wakandan technology that he uses to convert ordinary humans into Killmonger's merciless and fearsome Death Regiments.

KING CADAVER

The Resurrection Altar mutates one of Killmonger's most faithful minions into a sadistic psychic parasite, who enjoys violently plundering his victim's minds.
   Addicted to inflicting extreme psychological torment, King Cadaver is despised even by his own allies. He is killed by Venomm during Killmonger's final assault on Wakanda's capital city.

LORD KARNAJ

Killmonger's armies are equipped with state-of-the-art weapons maintained by the brutal Lord Karnaj. Highly trained in combat, the cruel quartermaster is a monster to his core. He gloats and revels in every death caused by the ordnance he provides. He dies during Killmonger's main offensive on the Wakandan Royal Palace.

SOMBRE

As high priest of the Resurrection Altar, Sombre is transformed by constant exposure to the shrine's all-pervading radiation. Fiendish and unfeeling, Sombre thrives on blood drained from human victims. The mutated vampire perishes when T'Challa hurls him into a quagmire and Sombre coldly refuses the Panther's offers of help.

MADAM SLAY

After Killmonger's death, his vengeful lover, Madam Slay, savagely attacks T'Challa. Using her power to command leopards and with the aid of her giant servant called Mute, she almost succeeds in killing the Black Panther. Slay later steals and preserves Killmonger's corpse using the Resurrection Altar and the Mandarin's arcane science to bring him back to life.

SALAMANDER K'RUEL

Stricken by Vibranium radiation from the sacred Great Mound, Salamander K'ruel sprouts toxic quills from sores and blisters all over his body. Enlisting with Killmonger's forces, K'ruel repeatedly tries—and fails—to kill the Panther, using both his unnatural powers and his sniper's bow and high-explosive arrows.

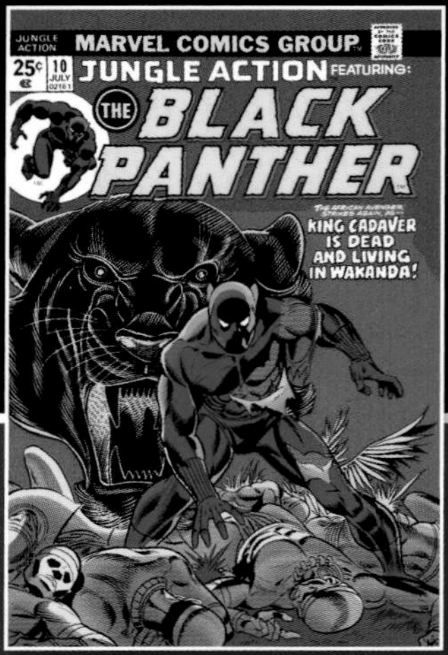
MARVEL COMICS GROUP
JUNGLE ACTION FEATURING:
THE BLACK PANTHER
KING CADAVER IS DEAD AND LIVING IN WAKANDA!

***Jungle Action* (Vol. 2) #10 (Jul. 1974)**

As king of Wakanda, T'Challa bears the burden of protecting his embattled people and ensuring the survival of the sacred Panther Cult. To preserve both he must also face the scientifically resurrected zombie legions of King Cadaver!

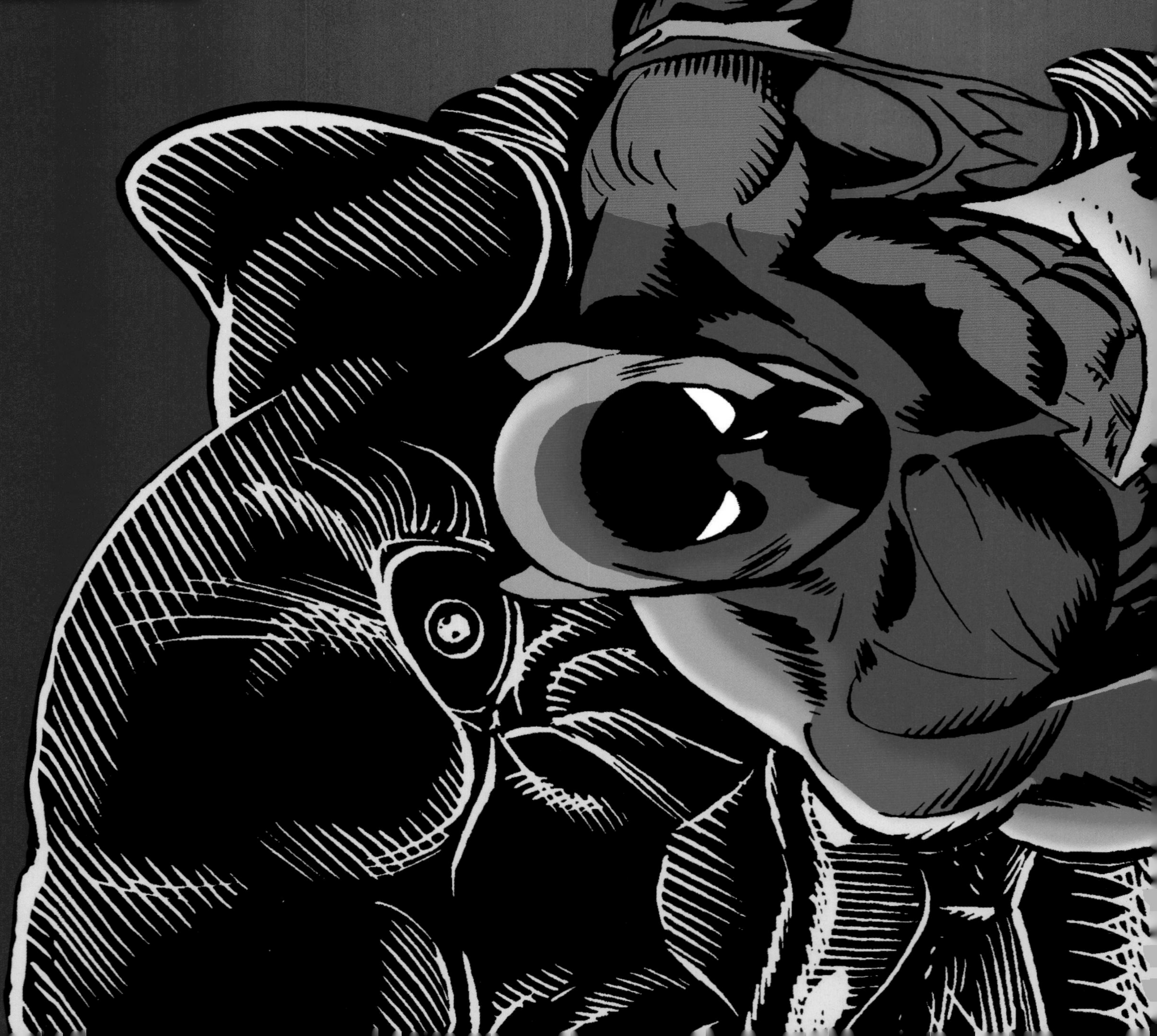

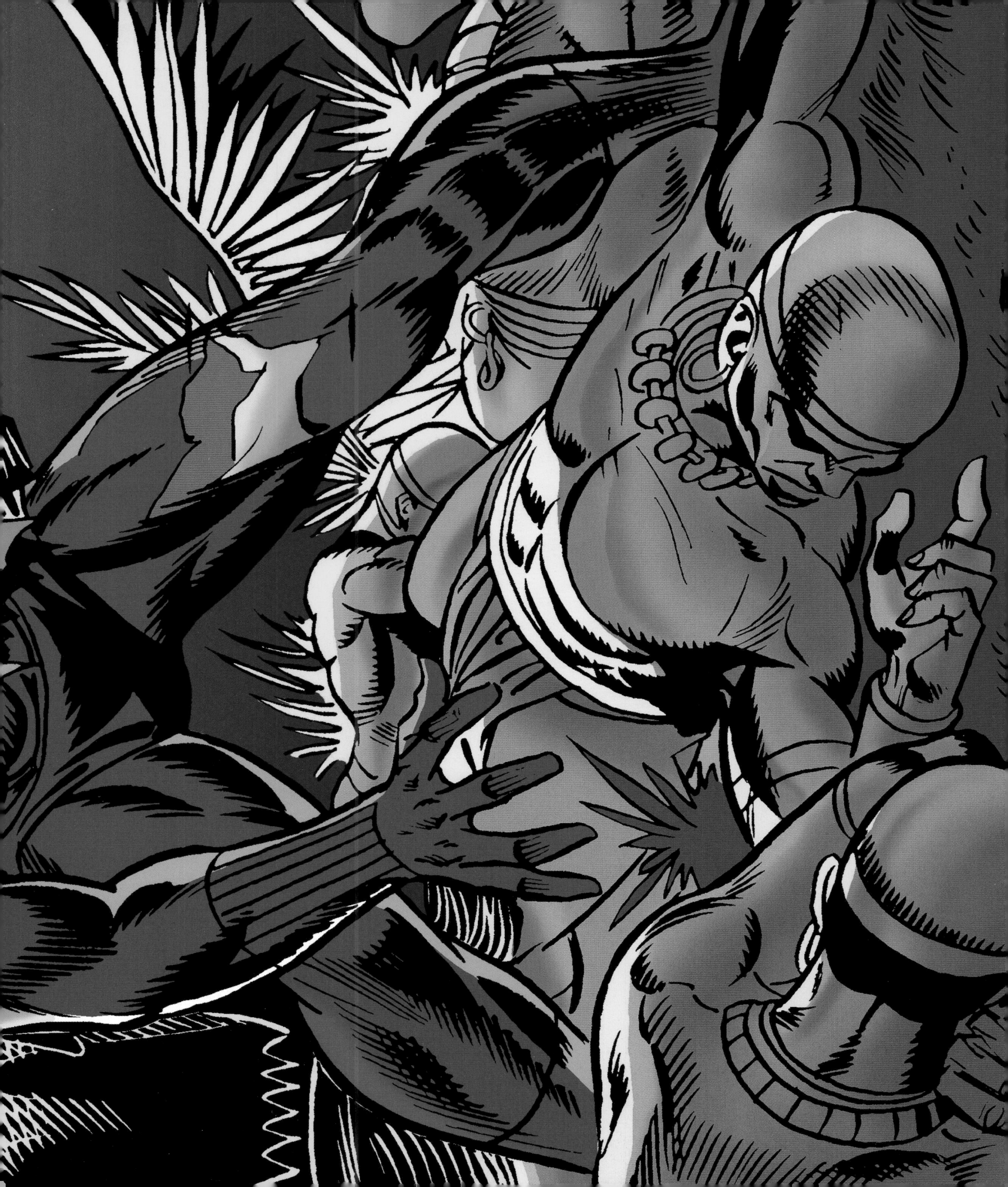

FRIENDS IN DEEDS

No king can govern alone and T'Challa depends on carefully chosen members of the Wakandan Inner Court Tribunal. These advisors and a few close friends provide him with important and decisive counsel in times of crisis.

TAKU

Taku is a voice of reason in T'Challa's inner circle. A brilliant computer scientist, he is both an international diplomat and the Wakandan Chief of Communications. During Killmonger's initial attacks on Wakanda, Taku's sensitive treatment turns the rebel's key lieutenant, Venomm, from a hostile prisoner into a useful ally.

W'KABI

Traditionally isolationist, W'Kabi is a member of the Taifa Ngao ("Shield of the Nation"), Chief of Security, and T'Challa's confidant in both state and personal matters. Losing an arm battling Killmonger, W'Kabi replaces the limb with weaponized bionic prosthetics. He sacrifices himself to save T'Challa and Shuri from the Devourer-of-Totems, Morlun.

KANTU

Kantu is taken in by Monica Lynne after Killmonger kills his father. The child tips the scales in the climactic battle between his father's murderer and T'Challa at Warrior Falls. Despite becoming a national hero, Kantu is deeply scarred by personal tragedy and becomes a dealer for crime boss Solomon Prey, before dying from a drug overdose.

MOKADI

Tracking Killmonger to Serpent Valley, T'Challa is intercepted by a strange little sprite called Mokadi. The king soon realizes that the impish creature's inquisitive, probing questions are intended to help clear T'Challa's head for the battle ahead. As Mokadi teleports around T'Challa, the Panther suspects he is a forest spirit of Wakandan folklore.

ZATAMA

An adviser on the Inner Court Tribunal, Zatama is, despite his youth, a fierce opponent of his country's growing militarization. He is killed by his lover—court handmaiden Tanzika—who frames Monica Lynne for the crime. The murder is part of an elaborate scheme to prevent Monica from marrying T'Challa, thus allowing Tanzika to become queen of Wakanda instead.

MENDINAO

Herbalist Mendinao officiates in the religious rituals that maintain T'Challa's Panther powers. He treats Wakandans who prefer traditional remedies to modern medical science. Despite his adherence to the old ways in his dress and manner, Mendinao is practiced in most of the therapeutic advances T'Challa has introduced to his nation.

MR. LITTLE

Abner Little deals in arcane artifacts. Deceptively adept and shrewd, the diminutive Soldier of Fortune helps T'Challa to secure King Solomon's Frogs— magical time machines. He remains to assist in a battle with the super-rich Collectors. Years later, he clashes with Iron Man before helping T'Challa thwart an attempt by his old enemy Princess Zanda to possess the time-bending Frogs.

KEVIN TRUBLOOD

Journalist Kevin Trublood helps T'Challa and Monica Lynne expose the cover-up of her sister's murder. After the Panther mysteriously vanishes, Kevin and Monica join forces to continue investigating the Dragon Circle Cult, and a romance between the two develops. When Kevin escorts Monica to the Wakandan Embassy months later, he unwittingly shocks T'Challa into rejecting the Dragons' programming and regaining his erased memories.

MONICA LYNNE

Love blooms for T'Challa after he saves the singer Monica Lynne from the Sons of the Serpent. He asks her to marry him, but her sister's murder, Killmonger's war, and T'Challa's subsequent brainwashing by the corrupt Dragon Circle group, forces them apart. Even after T'Challa's memory is restored, all attempts at reconciliation fail as the Panther's enemies continually use Monica as a pawn, forcing her to end the relationship.

THE COLLECTORS

His mind clouded and his memories altered by the Dragon Circle Cult, the Black Panther embarks upon globe-spanning escapades that take him to the edge of reason.

FAMILY TIES

T'Challa meets and befriends an old comrade of his paternal grandfather. Curiosities collector Abner Little seeks to return a time-bending brass frog—once belonging to Azzuri the Wise—to its rightful home, King Solomon's tomb. However, the new friends are too late to stop the artifact unleashing a killer from the past. Their voyage to the tomb is then interrupted when Zanda, a rival Collector, ambushes them.

Black Panther (Vol. 1) #1 (Jan. 1977)
Arrogant Zanda, a Collector, is used to getting what she wants, no matter who suffers for it.

Black Panther (Vol. 1) #4 (Jul. 1977)
The over-competitive Collectors trust no-one and continually seek to gain dominance over each other.

SAMURAI FOREVER

The billionaire Collectors—Zanda, Count Zorba, Colonel Pigman, and Silas Mourner—are ruthless bullies with seemingly infinite resources. To better enjoy their astounding possessions, they now want to live forever. T'Challa and Little are ordered to steal the Waters of Immortality from a lost colony of undying ancient Samurai. The Collectors know the Black Panther will comply because of the nuclear missiles they have aimed at the heart of hidden Wakanda.

Black Panther (Vol. 1) #1 (Jan. 1977)
The devastating Six Million Year Man proves that no-one should possess King Solomon's Frog.

FEAR THE FUTURE

The ensuing struggle again activates the frog, summoning a deadly being from six million years in the future. After subduing the creature, Panther, Little, and Zanda travel to King Solomon's lost tomb, seeking the frog's twin, which will return their prisoner to his own era. On arrival, the future-freak awakens, blasting them with energy beams, but a distraction allows T'Challa time to find and trigger the second frog, sending their assailant home. The struggle devastates the treasure-filled tomb, and a spiteful Zanda betrays her new allies to the rest of the Collectors.

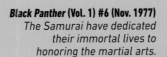
Black Panther (Vol. 1) #6 (Nov. 1977)
The Samurai have dedicated their immortal lives to honoring the martial arts.

"*In my dealing with* **competitors** *I've learned to prepare for* **any** *contingency.*"

ABNER LITTLE

Black Panther (Vol. 1) #1 (Jan. 1977) *Ancient family ties propel the Panther into a wild adventure thanks to a brass, magical frog.*

ASIAN ADVENTURES

After defeating ferocious Yeti-monsters and winning the trust of Earth's noblest warriors, T'Challa is welcomed by Lost Samurai leader Shinzu. When Abner Little tries to steal samples of the immortality water, Black Panther makes him return his ill-gotten prize and the warrior-cult allows their two "guests" to leave unharmed. T'Challa is utterly unaware that his sneaky companion has hidden away one tiny flask of the life-giving liquid.

Black Panther (Vol. 1) #7 (Jan. 1977) *T'Challa uses the Collectors' overwhelming greed against them and escapes their clutches.*

PRICE OF SUCCESS

Returning to the Collectors, T'Challa calls their nuclear bluff. When they learn that only one small sample of the life-giving waters exists, the Collectors turn on each other. In the chaotic struggle, the flask of water is destroyed, and T'Challa escapes in a commandeered helicopter. Ahead lies Wakanda, and an unexpected new crisis is about to unfold.

BAD COMPANY

"We're so good at celebrating the deaths of our enemies."

SOLOMON PREY

As hero and monarch, the Black Panther's activities bring him into conflict with many bizarre foes—super-powered villains, murderous malcontents, and superhuman warriors who cloak their crimes in dubious patriotism.

KIBER

While researching teleportation, scientist Frederick Kiber accidentally becomes a sentient protoplasm merged with his lab floor. Projecting holograms of his former self, Kiber consumes the life force of Wakandans who have been abducted and converted into pure energy. Invading the villain's island, T'Challa rescues Kiber's victims and condemns Kiber to starve in his ruined citadel.

ANTON PRETORIUS

South African magistrate Anton Pretorius kidnaps and enslaves Queen Mother Ramonda. Decades later, learning that his beloved stepmother is still alive, T'Challa risks an international incident to free her. Driven by guilt and paranoia, Pretorius hunts T'Challa with the help of government forces and an army of mercenaries. However, he fails to thwart the Panther's quest to save Ramonda.

DRAGON CIRCLE CULT

When Monica Lynne's sister Angela is murdered, T'Challa's investigation draws him into a war between the Ku Klux Klan and a Klan splinter faction, the Dragon Circle. The Dragons' leader, Reverend Addison Blackburn, is obsessed with power, and has his forces capture the Black Panther and subject him to extreme brainwashing. The process clouds T'Challa's memory of Angela, Monica, and fellow investigator Kevin Trublood, and he returns to Wakanda. Months later, a meeting with Kevin clears T'Challa's mind and the Panther tracks down and punishes the Dragons.

SOLOMON PREY

After graduating from Harvard, Solomon Prey returns to Wakanda, creating a criminal drug-dealing empire. Captivated by the psychotic killer Tanzika, Prey tries to destroy her archenemy, T'Challa, surgically transforming his own body to mimic the Pteranodons he controls. Ultimately, however, Prey perishes leading a reptile assault on Wakanda's capital city.

SUPREMACISTS OF AZANIA

Azania's apartheid-enforcing minority government brutalizes its black citizens, compelling the Panther Spirit to create a cat avatar to punish the white rulers. In retaliation, Azanian superteam the Supremacists is ordered to destroy Wakanda. However, despite an impressive show of force the team cannot overcome the power of the Black Panther.

White Avenger
Possesses super-strength, super-speed and heightened senses.

Barricade
Creates and projects forcefields.

Voortrekker
Weapons master and martial artist with superior tracking abilities.

Hungyr
Steals other people's strength and vitality to boost his own.

Captain Blaze
Projects flame and super-heated plasma.

Harrier
Wears weaponized armor supplemented with ballistic ordnance.

PENDRAGON'S BLACK KNIGHT

With Earth's ecology under attack from the evil Red Lord through his arcane force the Bane, Life's guardian, the Green Knight, mystically empowers the Knights of Pendragon to correct the imbalance. In Africa, the devastation wrought by the Bane demands the attention of the Black Panther.

HEART OF DARKNESS

T'Challa hosts a safari for Reed and Susan Richards on which they discover hippos slaughtered by poachers empowered by the demonic Bane. Joining forces with Pendragon Knights Kate McClellan, Ben Gallagher, and Union Jack, the heroes smash the poachers' gang and discover that the trail of atrocities leads to three international locations.

Knights of Pendragon (Vol. 1) #14 (Aug. 1991)
Even a pack of demonically possessed poachers cannot withstand the wrath of T'Challa and his allies.

Knights of Pendragon (Vol. 1) #1 (Sep. 1991)
En route to the House of Orchids, the Black Panther and Union Jack are attacked by Bane-controlled ninja.

HOUSE OF ORCHIDS

The Bane use unbridled capitalism, polluting technologies, and ancient magic to weaken the Earth in readiness for the coming of their diabolical Red Lord. When T'Challa and Union Jack journey to Hong Kong, they are attacked by Bane-controlled Ninjas and led into an unwinnable fight against the mystically mutated assassin Dolph.

FACE OF EVIL

With Pendragons divided between different Bane-triggered eco-crises, Black Panther and Union Jack are brutally injured by the Bane's horrific avatar. Realizing victory is impossible, Union Jack bundles the dying T'Challa onto his bike and whisks him to the nearest hospital. Turning to face super-thug Dolph once again, Jack is seemingly killed.

> *"Final battles are **never** really final, you know."*
> KING ARTHUR PENDRAGON

THE LAST BATTLE

Drawn to the Green Chapel of Avalon by the Green Knight, T'Challa's wounds are mystically healed. A resolute Black Panther returns to the fray and fights shoulder to shoulder beside valiant champions from all eras of Earth's history. Thanks to the dogged resistance of the planet's defenders, the voracious Red Lord is driven back once more.

CALL TO ARMS

From his hospital bed in Hong Kong, T'Challa sadly informs Kate that Union Jack has been killed after saving his life. However, as he speaks, the Green Knight issues a mystic invitation calling all his knights—living or otherwise—to assemble for their greatest mission.

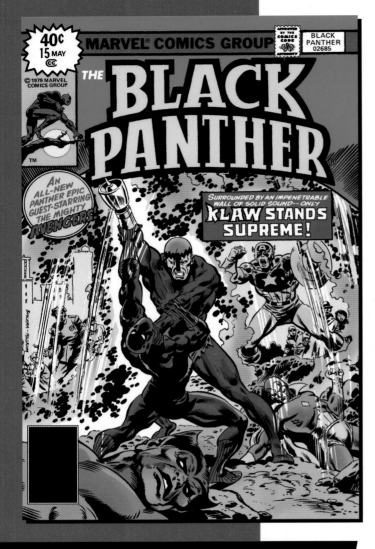

MAY 1979

BLACK PANTHER (VOL. 1) #15

T'CHALLA'S GREATEST ENEMY IS BACK, WITH THE AVENGERS AND NEW YORK IN HIS SIGHTS!

Returning to the U.S. to open Wakanda's first official embassy in New York, T'Challa's reunion with the Avengers is marred by the return of his most relentless foe, Ulysses Klaw. Accidentally revived from an amnesiac state by a street gang, the being of sound and fury uses his unwitting rescuers to regain freedom and full sonic power. Even the mighty Avengers seem powerless to stop him...

MAIN CHARACTERS
Black Panther (T'Challa) • Klaw

SUPPORTING CHARACTERS
Avengers (Beast, Vision, Captain America) • Taku • Wakabi • N'Yaga • Thunderbolts Gang (Herbie, Levon, Jackie)

MAIN LOCATIONS
New York City • Wakandan Embassy • Harlem

1 As the Avengers prepare to ship an imprisoned and comatose Klaw to Wakanda, the villain awakens and counterattacks. Manipulating a gang of hapless street thugs to help free him, Klaw assaults the assembled heroes—Black Panther, Captain America, the Vision, and the Beast—with rampaging solid-sound animal constructs.

3 Fully reinvigorated, Klaw breaks his bonds and ruthlessly turns on his enslaved minions. The Vision phases through the dock floor to save them but even his power cannot halt the resurgent villain...

2 Re-energized, Klaw has his sonically created pawns form an impenetrable sound bubble. As the Avengers struggle to get inside the dome, the undying fiend gathers strength from the cacophony and chaos raging around him.

4 Realizing Black Panther has a plan to defeat Klaw, the Vision engages the villain in punishing hand-to-hand combat to buy time. As the fight intensifies, the android Avenger remains all too aware that each blow he lands makes his enemy stronger, and brings them ever closer to a devastating sonic meltdown.

"Fool! I don't need my soni-claw to defeat the likes of you!"

KLAW

5 The Vision's valiant stalling tactics succeed. When Wakandan envoys Taku and N'Yaga arrive with sound-damping Vibranium gloves devised by T'Challa, the tide of battle swiftly turns. The Black Panther rips apart the sound wall and in the brutal fight that follows, forces Klaw to give ground.

6 As Klaw oscillates out of control and nears explosive detonation, the Panther drags the villain into the river. With the water damping the escalating sound energy, T'Challa turns Klaw's own soni-claw on him, forcing an implosion that disperses the sound being throughout the sea.

PANTHER'S QUEST

After decades believing he is alone, T'Challa, the Orphan King, learns that his cherished, long-missing stepmother, Ramonda, is alive. The only problem is that she is living in South Africa, which is suffering under the oppressively hostile apartheid regime.

MISSING MOTHER

T'Challa is three years old when his adored stepmother, Ramonda, vanishes. Neither his father T'Chaka, nor anybody else at court mentions her name again. Years later, however, T'Challa is told that she left her family for a white man in South Africa. Then one day a message arrives from an anonymous source: Ramonda lives.

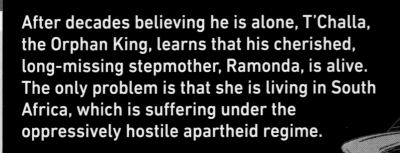

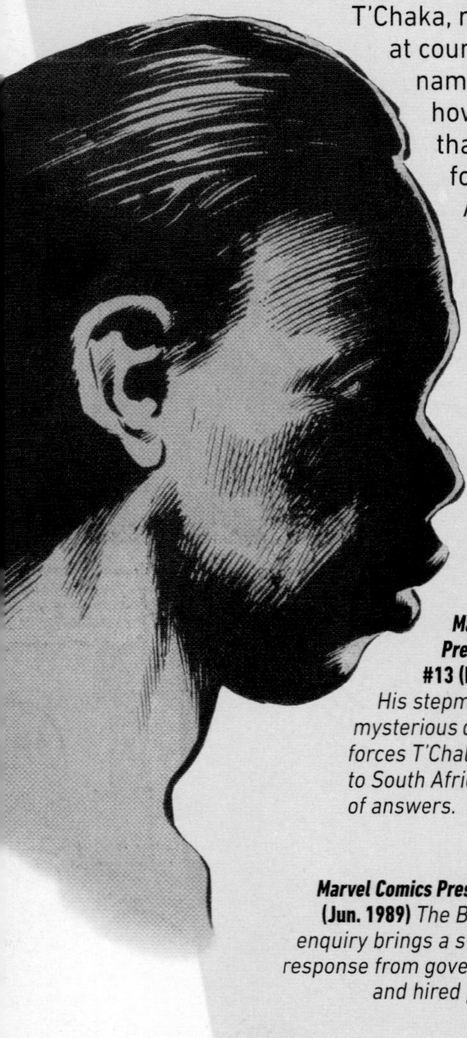

Marvel Comics Presents (Vol. 1) #13 (Feb. 1989) *His stepmother's mysterious disappearance forces T'Challa to travel to South Africa in search of answers.*

Marvel Comics Presents (Vol. 1) #21 (Jun. 1989) *The Black Panther's enquiry brings a swift and brutal response from government troops and hired paramilitaries.*

Marvel Comics Presents (Vol. 1) #31 (Nov. 1989) *Searching for his missing stepmother, T'Challa encounters hostility at every turn.*

THROUGH THE BARRICADES

The apartheid regime has been trying to destabilize Wakanda for decades, but T'Challa clandestinely enters South Africa, aware that his skin color marks him out as an enemy of the state. Unsure if Ramonda selfishly left, or was somehow taken, T'Challa's planned meeting with an informer is interrupted by mercenaries with orders to kill him...

Marvel Comics Presents **(Vol. 1) #32 (Nov. 1989)** *Tackled by the Panther on an escalator, the mercenary called Strike confirms the location of T'Challa's mysterious enemy.*

UNDER SIEGE

After enduring horrific injuries at the hands of paramilitaries and state forces, T'Challa meets impoverished goldminer Zanti Chikane. Despite daily harassment from state soldiers and living under atrocious conditions, Zanti assists T'Challa in his search, which takes him from beleaguered townships to the whites-only tourist enclave of Johannesburg. All the while, government forces and a concealed foe's hired goons hinder their every step.

FORBIDDEN LOVE

With his power and reputation under threat, Pretorius acts with increasing desperation. He futilely attempts to hide his perilous secret, keep possession of Ramonda, and destroy his ever-nearing nemesis T'Challa.

Marvel Comics Presents **(Vol. 1) #25 (Aug. 1989)** *After decades of leading a comfortable, secure life, Pretorius' world begins to crumble around him.*

Marvel Comics Presents **(Vol. 1) #36 (Dec. 1989)** *No trap nor brute employed by Anton Pretorius seem able to prevent the Panther from reaching the Magistrate's heavily protected household.*

THE TIES THAT BIND

T'Challa's hidden adversary and Ramonda's captor is revealed as Anton Pretorius, South Africa's Magistrate of Communications. His actions break all his apartheid government's strict laws on interracial relationships. Thanks to the Black Panther's actions, the Magistrate's own colleagues grow suspicious.

MOTHER AND CHILD REUNION

Finally freed by her beloved stepson, Ramonda reveals how, decades earlier, Pretorius captured and imprisoned her in his mansion after she had attended her father's funeral. The corrupt Magistrate's attempts to make his captive love him were met with fierce resistance. After her stepson liberates her, a resolute Ramonda deals her defeated jailer his greatest injury: complete rejection.

Marvel Comics Presents **(Vol. 1) #37 (Dec. 1989)** *After years of imprisonment, Ramonda rejects the cowardly Pretorius in a very direct way.*

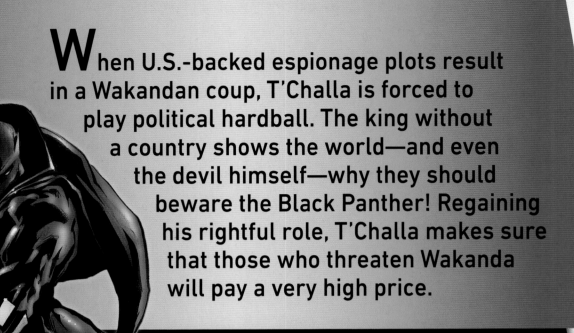

When U.S.-backed espionage plots result in a Wakandan coup, T'Challa is forced to play political hardball. The king without a country shows the world—and even the devil himself—why they should beware the Black Panther! Regaining his rightful role, T'Challa makes sure that those who threaten Wakanda will pay a very high price.

HEAVY SITS THE CROWN

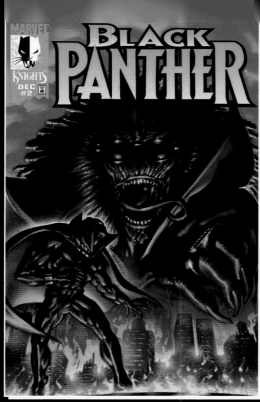

Black Panther (Vol. 3) #2 (Dec. 1998)
T'Challa is back in action, back in the U.S., and backed into a corner against the Devil himself, Mephisto.

Black Panther (Vol. 3) #36 (Dec. 2001)
Celebrating 35 years of Black Panther adventures with a glimpse of what the next quarter century holds for him.

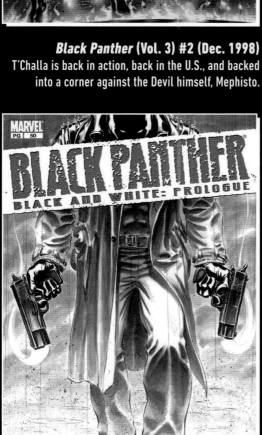

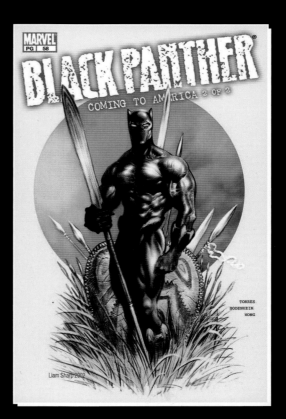

Black Panther (Vol. 3) #50 (Dec. 2002)
As T'Challa vanishes from public life, a new gun-toting Black Panther prowls New York City's streets.

Black Panther (Vol. 3) #58 (Jun. 2003)
T'Challa stalks New York City as he investigates the murder of fellow African king Akaje of Dakenia.

ENEMY OF THE STATE II

Discovering that Wakanda's recent economic and political problems are seemingly instigated by the U.S. intelligence community, T'Challa takes action. After months of planning, Black Panther's elaborate scheme to smoke out the real culprits destabilizing his country enters the final stages.

*"To live, to die, to rule again... the Panther must walk **alone**."*

T'CHALLA

MENDING FENCES

When U.S. senator Kamal Rakim asks Tony Stark to investigate a murdered gangster with C.I.A. connections, Iron Man sees an opportunity to rebuild his friendship with the Black Panther. Relations between them have been strained ever since Stark bought out the Wakanda Design Group during the economic crash T'Challa had engineered to counter Achebe and Killmonger's coups in Wakanda.

Black Panther **(Vol. 3) #41 (Apr. 2002)**
The Black Panther shockingly and imperiously severs all ties with his Avenger allies.

DEADLY SECRETS

T'Challa conceals many secrets. One is a time-displaced future self: a jolly, devil-may-care Black Panther dying of a brain tumor. Another is his own recent incurable brain injury. A third is discovering that XCon—a clandestine coalition of international intelligence agencies—has gone rogue and caused Wakanda's current woes. More alarmingly, XCon has also successfully replaced Canada's prime minister and the U.S. president, effectively taking over control of North America.

Black Panther **(Vol. 3) #41 (Apr. 2002)** *T'Challa and his future self devise one last ploy to confuse their enemies and allies alike—swapping uniforms.*

Black Panther (Vol. 3) #42 (May 2002) Stark reels as he finds T'Challa has taken over his company and bugged Avengers Mansion.

Black Panther (Vol. 3) #44 (Jul. 2002) *Finally up to speed, Iron Man tackles XCon's new boss, the White Wolf.*

BACK FROM THE FUTURE

Using King Solomon's time-warping brass frogs, XCon has quietly replaced world leaders with their future selves, each programmed to carry out XCon's commands. All T'Challa's gambits—manipulating global stock markets, seizing control of Stark Enterprises, annexing parts of Canada, and apparently bugging Avengers Mansion—are complex tests to determine whether Iron Man is also part of the conspiracy...willing or otherwise. Unknown to Stark, a future version of himself is also on the loose, brainwashed by XCon and wearing stolen stealth armor.

Black Panther (Vol. 3) #45 (Aug. 2002)
Future Iron Man's stealth armor could not detect that his opponent was not the present-day Panther but the time-displaced T'Challa.

BEWARE THE WOLF

After a series of fierce clashes between Iron Man, Wolverine, Alpha Flight, and the Black Panther, Stark realizes T'Challa's true intentions, but finds his royal rival still one step ahead of him. XCon no longer exists, having been infiltrated, gutted, and taken over by T'Challa's adopted brother, Hunter, a.k.a. the White Wolf, as retaliation for XCon's attacks on Wakanda. Hunter now intends to use XCon's remnants for his own purposes. However, even his devoted *Hatut Zeraze* cannot handle the power of an enraged Tony Stark, who takes them down.

DOUBLE INDEMNITY

Rushing off to confront T'Challa, Stark is unaware that his future self is sneaking into the White House, or that another Black Panther is out to stop Stark's stealth-armored doppelgänger. A savage battle breaks out as T'Challa and Stark's future doubles duel to the death in the skies above the White House, with their present-day counterparts watching in horror. The brutal outcome shatters XCon's secret substitution scheme. It also compels the real-time Black Panther and Iron Man to reappraise their friendship and how their win-at-all-cost arrogance brought the world to the brink of disaster.

Black Panther (Vol. 3) #45 (Aug. 2002)
In the aftermath of their doubles' battle, the real-time Stark and T'Challa wonder if their strained friendship can survive, knowing how little they trust each other.

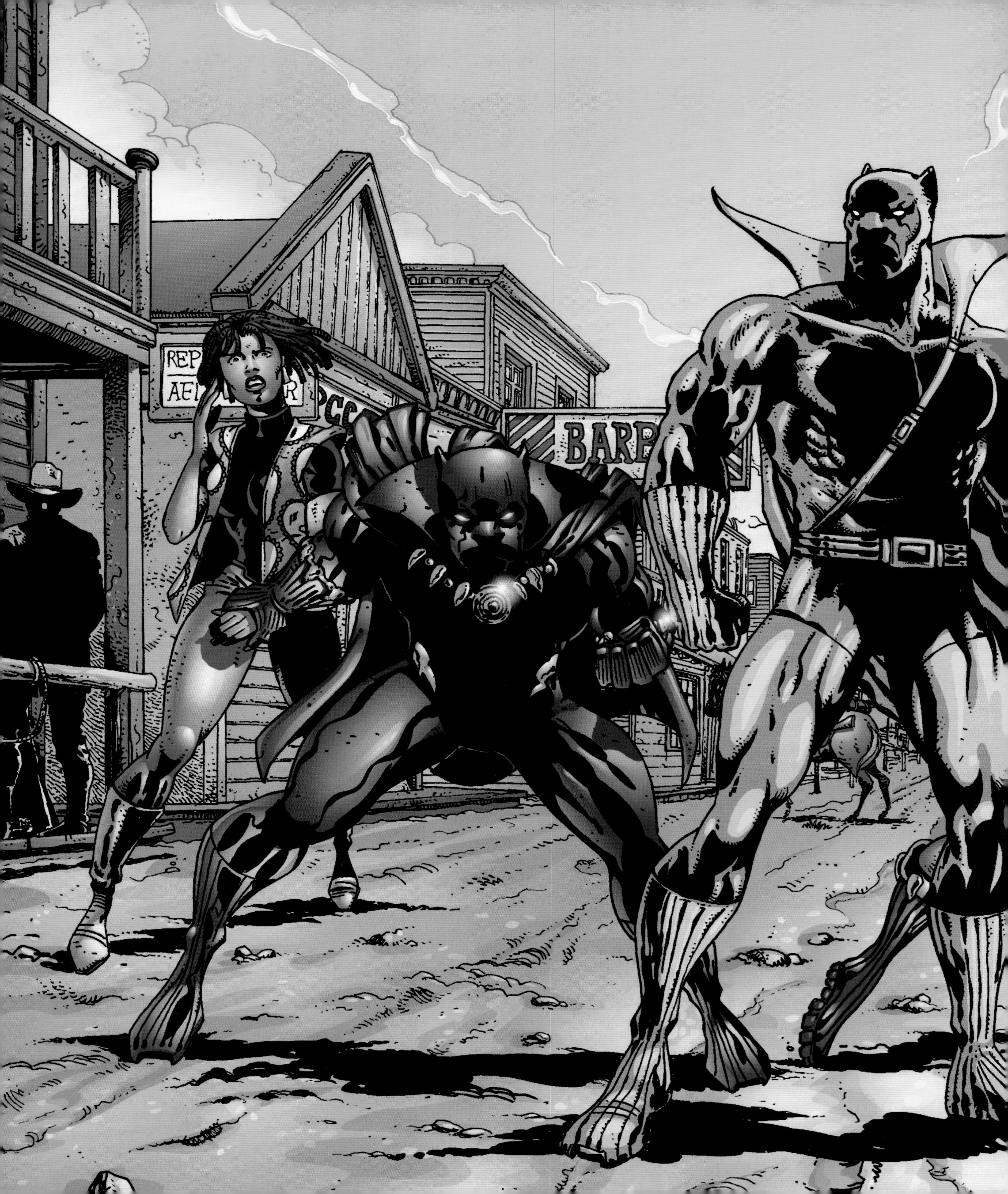
REP
BARB

Black Panther (Vol. 3) #46 (Sep. 2002)
King Solomon's time-hopping frogs maroon T'Challa, his future self, and a posse of pals, including Monica Lynne and Queen Divine Justice, in the Wild West in 1875. Here they join forces with Marvel Comics' greatest cowboy heroes to stop the imminent twilight of the Asgardian Gods.

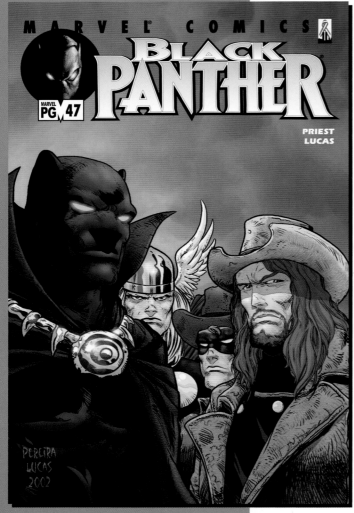

MARVEL® COMICS

BLACK PANTHER

MARVEL PG 47

PRIEST
LUCAS

PEREIRA
LUCAS
2002

BLACK PANTHER (VOL.3) #47

T'CHALLA IS HIJACKED ACROSS TIME AND DROPPED INTO A DEATH DUEL BETWEEN GODS!

After saving the world from XCon's elaborate time-warping scheme, T'Challa, his future self, and a close group of associates are stranded in 1875 Texas. They soon discover the evil god Loki is attempting to eliminate his Asgardian race.

OCTOBER 2002

MAIN CHARACTERS
Black Panther • Future Black Panther • Thor

SUPPORTING CHARACTERS
Two Gun Kid • Rawhide Kid • Kid Colt • Sundance • Everett Ross • Queen Divine Justice • Monica Lynne • Henry Peter Gyrich

MAIN LOCATIONS
Buzzard Gulch • Texas, 1875 • Asgard

1 In the American Wild West, Loki has stolen Idunn's Apples of Immortality, which grant the Asgardian gods their near-immortality, youth, and vigor. When the two T'Challas and their 21st century comrades arrive—courtesy of King Solomon's Frogs—they join a feeble, aging Thor and some cowboy heroes in an urgent quest for the fabled fruits.

2 One of Idunn's Apples is hidden aboard a train rolling into sleepy Buzzard Gulch. By the time Black Panther and his posse forcibly board the magnificent "Iron Horse," the Prince of Evil has packed it with his monstrous Troll allies. Loki then magically propels the train towards Asgard and the slowly expiring gods.

*"For **nigh** is the **day** of thy reckoning!"*

THOR

3 As Loki gloats over the sleeping, imprisoned form of All-Father Odin, below the Eternal Citadel a surprise turn of events threatens to derail his plans. Both T'Challas and their unlikely team slowly whittle down Loki's occupying forces, before preparing to launch an all-out frontal assault.

4 With his plot unraveling, Loki furiously confronts the mortal invaders. Future T'Challa boldly attacks, using his cat-like speed to deprive the villain of the Golden Apple. Future Panther passes it on to his cowboy comrades in a race to save the dying Thor.

5 After one bite of the goddess Idunn's Apple of Immortality, the frail Thunder God is restored to his full majestic power. Enraged and invigorated, Thor joins the Panthers and their allies in mopping up the invading trolls and capturing a stunned Loki.

6 With the God of Evil defeated and order restored to the Eternal Realm, the two T'Challas bid farewell to their Wild West allies. They make ready to escort home the time-displaced party of mismatched adventurers—thanks to the marvels of Asgardian magic.

MADE IN AMERICA

Although an African king, T'Challa maintains close ties with the U.S. To the Panther, the country is a safe place to shelter Wakandan exiles and is also filled with heroes ready to battle beside him, no matter how difficult the struggle.

DEADPOOL

Undying mutant mercenary Wade Wilson adds layers of chaos to a simple abduction mission after a spiteful Achebe —masquerading as T'Challa— hires the unpredictable anti-hero to steal a pet leopard. The beast belongs to Killmonger, who has replaced the Black Panther in the Avengers after T'Challa vanishes into his electronic jungle to recuperate from a recent near-death experience. When the Avengers invade Wakanda, Deadpool's manic interference and Killmonger's distracted instability allow T'Challa to find a subtle and unlikely solution to the growing international crisis.

EVERETT K. ROSS

Timid, self-conscious civil servant Everett Ross is assigned as State Department Liaison to King T'Challa and is immediately drawn into several perilous situations with the Black Panther's entourage. These terrifying incidents include being used and abused by Mephisto and becoming an unwilling regent of Wakanda. Surviving these experiences makes him the U.S.'s go-to expert on all things Wakandan.

QUEEN DIVINE JUSTICE

At the behest of the Black Panther, Jabari princess Ce'Athauna Asira Davin is secretly raised in the U.S. by Wakandan agents as Chanté Giovanni Brown. Orphaned as an infant after her parents, rulers of the outlawed White Gorilla Cult, perish trying to overthrow Wakanda's ruling Panther Cult, Chanté's life is spared and she is sent into exile. Years later, Chanté—now calling herself Queen Divine Justice— is retrieved by T'Challa who reveals her regal heritage and inducts her into his *Dora Milaje*.

VIBRAXAS

N'Kano becomes an orphan when a Vibranium experiment kills his researcher parents. Afflicted with uncontrollable vibrational powers, he is saved by King T'Challa, who builds N'Kano a harness to stabilize his powers, before sending him to the U.S. to train with the Fantastic Force. Returning as Vibraxas, N'Kano has a platonic— but forbidden—friendship with Queen Divine Justice.

IRON FIST

Living weapon Danny Rand is Iron Fist, the Earth-bound champion of mystical city K'un-Lun. He meets T'Challa through Daredevil and Luke Cage, becoming a trusted ally. When Iron Fist is possessed by the villainous Black Dragon, T'Challa attempts to stop him, but is beaten so severely he develops a brain tumor. Unaware of the harm he has caused, Danny eventually shakes off the saurian's influence, and helps Black Panther defeat the dragon.

KASPER COLE

Policeman Kevin "Kasper" Cole steals an old Black Panther uniform to conceal his clandestine war against the 66 Bridges Gang and the corrupt cops running his precinct. Later, T'Challa and Killmonger both teach Cole the necessary lore to become a true Black Panther. After narrowly failing the ritual, Cole becomes crusading Panther Cult acolyte the White Tiger.

JUNTA

Manuel Diego Armand Vicente uses his gravity powers as a mercenary for various international intelligence agencies. After he destabilizes Wakanda and puts Achebe on the throne, his paymasters turn on him. In response, "Junta" works with T'Challa to bring down the masterminds behind the operation. This brings him into an alliance with vigilante team the Crew.

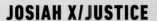

JOSIAH X/JUSTICE

Josiah Bradley's father, Isaiah, was the U.S.'s first African-American Super-Soldier. After several tours in Vietnam, Josiah is court-martialed and imprisoned. He escapes and hides out in New York City's Little Mogadishu district. There he becomes a Muslim cleric and, as Justice, joins hero team the Crew to clean the streets of drug dealers.

SGT. FRANCIS BARTHOLOMEW TORK

Undercover cop Sgt. Tork is an old associate of T'Challa. He assists Kevin Cole in his impersonation of the Black Panther until he is apparently assassinated by his fellow officers. The death is faked, allowing the unconventional law officer to work covertly against the corrupt cops and clear Cole's name.

WAR MACHINE

Bankrupt James Rhodes sells his War Machine armor. When his sister Jeanette dies of a drug overdose, Rhodes uses his Super Hero experience, Stark Industries business contacts, and fragments of dismantled tech to hunt the drug dealers and the corporation that secretly sponsors them. This brings him into contact with the Crew, a group of like-minded individuals with similar goals. Rhodes eventually resumes his role as War Machine and is later killed battling Thanos.

ORIGIN

Following T'Challa's clash with the Collectors, King Solomon's Frogs pluck a Black Panther from 10 years in the future and maroon him in the present. This "Future Panther" gradually makes his way to his former kingdom of Wakanda. Several months before Achebe's coup, present-day T'Challa meets his double and learns that the newcomer is dying from a blood clot in his brain. When Future Panther lapses into a coma, T'Challa places him in cryogenic suspension while seeking a solution. The future T'Challa is hidden in the remote ice palace of the rebellious Jabari, where he remains, until a battle with M'Baku the Man-Ape exposes him.

The wonder years
When Black Panther first meets his elder incarnation, the present-day king becomes fixated on the time-displaced hero's imminent death. Future T'Challa reveals nothing of the years to come, but strongly advises his younger self to enjoy life. Instead, the present-day T'Challa breaks off his engagement to Monica Lynne and strives even harder to make Wakanda totally secure.

"We war-weary Wakandans share but a fleeting moment of joy and song!"

FUTURE T'CHALLA

Catnapped
After the frozen future T'Challa is placed aboard a N'Yami cruiser, he is stolen by criminal geneticist Deadly Nightshade. She revives and experiments on him, concocting a serum that reverses many of his agonizing symptoms. He awakens as a flamboyant swashbuckler, completely different to his younger, grimmer self.

FUTURE PANTHER

In a life full of incredible adventures, the brooding, responsibility-burdened T'Challa never expects to encounter a future incarnation of himself so unlike anything he could imagine. However, fate restores to the world a dying, devil-may-care version of the Black Panther as he might have been, or may yet become...

Although from the future, T'Challa wears his original black cloth Panther garb.

Time bandits

Instrumental in helping end the civil war between Wakandan tribes, Future T'Challa then aids his younger self in a complex scheme to prevent maverick intelligence agency XCon from conquering the U.S. The plan reunites the future Black Panther with old ally Abner Little and seductive enemy Princess Zanda of Narobia. The three are joined by U.S. State Department agent Everett Ross to hunt down the missing twin of King Solomon's Frog.

Future Panther keeps in touch with his other self via a concealed radio system.

Panther gauntlets only retain climbing claws and stun-gas emitters.

DOUBLE TROUBLES

Despite the future T'Challa possessing extrasensory perception and telepathy, he cannot penetrate the mind of his stoic younger self. He never realizes that, while he and Deadly Nightshade are quelling tribal uprisings, present-day T'Challa is battling a mind-controlled Iron Fist. The ferocious fight leaves present-day T'Challa with life-threatening head injuries and, inevitably, a fatal brain condition similar to that of his future self.

Ghosts at the funeral

On returning from an adventure in the Old West, Nightshade's serum stops working and future T'Challa collapses. Despite heroic measures, he again becomes comatose and is placed in stasis. When his slumbering body is killed by M'Baku the Man-Ape, present-day T'Challa is forced to radically rethink his future, and vanishes from Wakanda.

SCHEMERS, DREAMERS, DEMONS, AND REDEEMERS

Black Panther always puts Wakanda first. Realizing there is no safety in isolation, T'Challa leaves Wakanda to defend his country from beyond its borders as a hero and Avenger. However, old and new enemies are forever ready to exploit his land and people.

ACHEBE

Reverend Achebe spearheads a coup that ousts and exiles the Black Panther. Mystically aided by Mephisto, and backed by American spymasters and the criminal intelligence agency XCon, the increasingly insane cleric wreaks havoc across the country once his allies desert him. When the coup fails, Achebe manages to escape justice and returns often to plague T'Challa.

PRIESTLORD GHAUR

Despotic religious leader Ghaur presides over the hidden Deviant nation, hungering for his subjects to be Earth's ruling race. His human-seeming infant daughter is a shameful embarrassment whom Ghaur wants eliminated, but she is under the Black Panther's protection. Despite having challenged the might of the Avengers, Eternals, and X-Men, the terrifying Ghaur cannot intimidate T'Challa, who declares war on the Deviants. The U.S. and Atlantis become embroiled in the escalating conflict before a cunning solution—faking the child's death—ends hostilities.

MALICE II (NAKIA)

Disgraced *Dora Milaje* Nakia is infatuated with T'Challa and targets anyone close to him. Physically enhanced by magic and Killmonger's Resurrection Altar, she hunts down and tortures those she sees as rivals for T'Challa's affection. After killing Nikki Adams and capturing T'Challa, whom she drugs in an effort to gain his love, Malice is outwitted by the Panther and vanishes.

BLACK DRAGON

Sorcerous shape-shifting dragon Chiantang dies trying to destroy the city of K'un-Lun. When he is revived by Nightshade, Black Dragon turns his magic and rage upon Earth. After devastating New York City and Wakanda, the saurian is deprived of his power in a catastrophic clash with Black Panther and Iron Fist, and is turned over to T'Challa's subjects for judgment.

NIGHTSHADE

Tilda Johnson is a career criminal who uses her scientific brilliance and ruthless ambition to dominate men and steal. She specializes in seduction and metamorphic transformation, but is repeatedly defeated by Captain America, Falcon, Luke Cage, and Iron Fist, among others. Nightshade clashes with the Black Panther and later spitefully resurrects his foe Black Dragon, before stealing T'Challa's most carefully guarded secret—his cryogenically frozen future self. After helping fix the crisis she created, Nightshade escapes custody and remains at large.

MEPHISTO

Demon-Lord Mephisto lives to corrupt powerful souls such as Thor, Silver Surfer, and Spider-Man using convoluted schemes intended to torment heroes to breaking point.

Empowering Achebe to seize Wakanda, Mephisto demands T'Challa's soul as the price for saving the beleaguered nation. However, when T'Challa agrees, Mephisto is unable to bear the spiritual burden of the unified spirits of every Black Panther who has ever lived. As a result, the archvillain furiously relinquishes his claim.

NIGHTMARE

Demonic Nightmare thrives on terror generated by sleeping minds, constantly testing Earth's magical champions, including Doctor Strange, Ghost Rider, and Sleepwalker. When rivals depose him from his Splinter Realm, Nightmare attacks T'Challa as he lies dying, hoping to steal his connection to the Panther Spirit as a beacon to regain his ethereal home. Thanks to the heroes Moon Knight and Doctor Voodoo, T'Challa escapes the trap and, in the process, frees many Wakandan souls held in the dream lord's bondage.

GODS AND MONSTERS

In an African culture like Wakanda, where ancient gods still thrive and animal spirits commune with select mortals, many rival cults develop over the centuries to challenge the preeminence of the Panther Spirit. However, even gods do not live forever...

WHITE GORILLA CULT

Based in Wakanda's cold, mountainous Jabari-Lands, a cult devoted to brutal survival has evolved around the carnivorous white gorillas who roam the icy slopes. Over the years, Jabari shamans discover that a worshiper can gain unnatural strength and power by killing a gorilla and drinking its blood.

Jungle Action (Vol. 2) #13 (Jan. 1975)

THE ORISHAS

The original gods of Africa are the Orishas—Thoth, Bast, Kokou, Mujaji, and Ptah—mighty beings who influence every aspect of life for millions of people. However, following the destruction and resurrection of the multiverse, Wakanda's shamans and priests realize that their pantheon of patrons has gone missing...

Black Panther (Vol. 6) #13 (Jun. 2017)

LION GOD CULT

When the Pharaohs fell, Hathor-Sekhmet relocated to Central Africa. His Lion God cultists never attain the heights of Bast's worshipers, perhaps due to Sekhmet's desire for a human sacrifice before revealing himself on Earth. When T'Challa brings Wakanda onto the world stage, the Lion God targets him and the Avengers, hoping to steal the Panther God's secrets.

Black Panther (Vol. 1) #114 (Aug. 1973)

CAT'S CRADLE OF CIVILIZATION

The dominant tribe of Wakanda has worshiped Bast—the great Panther God—for millennia. One of the fabled Orisha, Bast brings knowledge and wisdom to Bashenga's tribe and the two form a pact to ensure their continuing dominance.

In the distant past, Bast reigns in Lower Egypt while her feline brother Hathor-Sekhmet rules Upper Egypt. The twins battle constantly and eventually Bast withdraws, establishing an unbroken theological relationship with the Panther Cult that continues to this day. This bond is clearly seen in the many magnificent Panther icons gracing Wakanda.

Fantastic Four (Vol. 1) #607 (Aug. 2012)

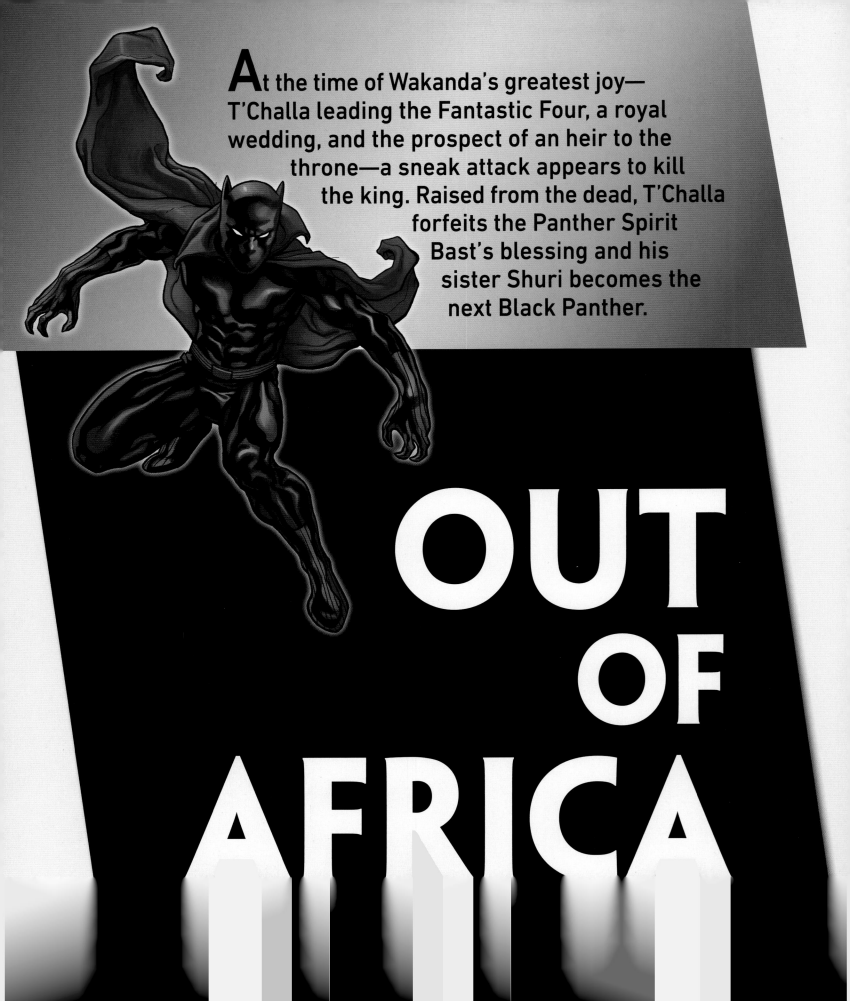

At the time of Wakanda's greatest joy— T'Challa leading the Fantastic Four, a royal wedding, and the prospect of an heir to the throne—a sneak attack appears to kill the king. Raised from the dead, T'Challa forfeits the Panther Spirit Bast's blessing and his sister Shuri becomes the next Black Panther.

OUT OF AFRICA

Black Panther (Vol. 4) #1 (Apr. 2005)
A new era for the Great Cat begins with the
secret history of never-conquered Wakanda.

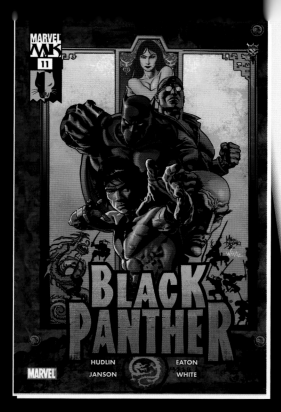

Black Panther (Vol. 4) #11 (Feb. 2008)
Earth's most sinister villain offers his daughter as
T'Challa's potential bride and queen of Wakanda!

Black Panther (Vol. 4) #34 (Mar. 2008)
T'Challa and Ororo relive the history of America's
Civil Rights Movement on a Skrull planet.

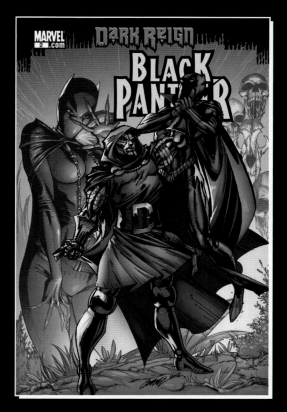

Black Panther (Vol. 5) #2 (May 2009)
With T'Challa seemingly assassinated, Shuri must protect
Wakanda—if the Panther Spirit deems her worthy.

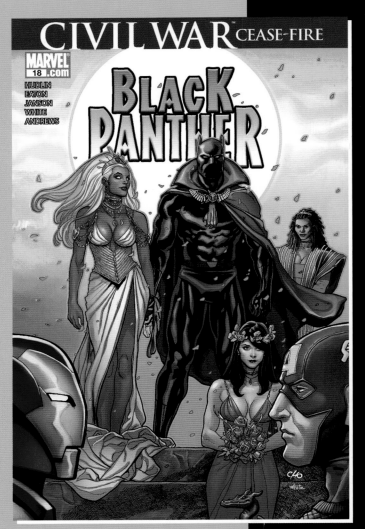

CIVIL WAR CEASE-FIRE

MARVEL
18
.com

HUDLIN
EATON
JANSON
WHITE
ANDREWS

BLACK PANTHER (VOL. 4) #18

WITNESS THE GRANDEST ROYAL WEDDING OF THE CENTURY.

On the firm insistence of Queen Mother Ramonda, T'Challa undertakes a global search to find a bride and secure an heir to the throne of Wakanda. After meeting and declining many candidates, the bachelor king realizes he can only be truly happy with his first love—the weather-shaping mutant hero named Storm.

SEPTEMBER 2006

MAIN CHARACTERS
Black Panther (T'Challa) • Ororo Iqadi T'Challa née Munroe

SUPPORTING CHARACTERS
Munroe family • Iron Man • Captain America • X-Men • Secret Avengers • Fantastic Four • Inhuman royal family • The Watcher • Nearly every hero in the Marvel Universe

MAIN LOCATIONS
Central Wakanda • Royal Palace

1 Despite the turmoil engulfing the U.S. due to the unpopular enforcement of the Superhuman Registration Act, T'Challa and Storm's comrades and acquaintances agree to a ceasefire in their ongoing civil war to attend the wedding. Friends-turned-enemies (and estranged family members) abide by the truce to avoid spoiling the couple's big day.

2 Despite the best of intentions, faction leaders Captain America and Iron Man are unable to reconcile their differences, even on such a special occasion. Rather than contravene the neutrality of Wakanda, or spoil the wedding, both heroes depart the country before the ceremony begins.

3 The surprise arrival of cosmic intelligence-gatherer Uatu the Watcher confirms to all guests and global audiences that this is an alliance of world—if not universal—significance.

*"The Panther God has **blessed this couple**. Pity **anyone** who stands in the path of their happiness."*

QUEEN MOTHER RAMONDA

4 A Black Panther's wedding is like no other. After the bride and groom have exchanged vows, the Panther God must give her own assessment and blessing. The ordeal involves transportation to the Celestial Plane and a painstaking examination of Ororo's soul.

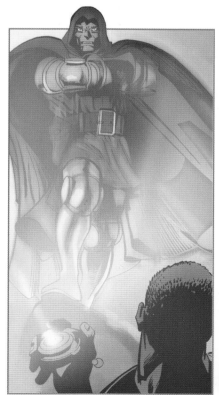

6 Once the joyous festivities conclude, the happy couple receive far more ominous congratulations. Former Latverian monarch and temporary prisoner of Hell, Doctor Doom, forgives the newlyweds for not inviting him, but departs with a cryptic warning that fills them with unease. T'Challa and Ororo cannot begin to conceive the plans the malign monarch has for them and Wakanda.

5 Happily, the new queen is found satisfactory in the eyes of Wakanda's godly guardian and is returned to the Earthly Realm to enjoy a spectacular wedding feast with her new husband. As is customary on such occasions, the evening concludes with a good-natured Super Hero brawl.

STORM

Storm crushes evil and dispenses salvation with equal force and passion. An indomitable warrior and skilful leader, she hates resorting to violence and would rather use her incredible mutant powers to better lives and nurture the planet's embattled ecology.

ORIGIN

Ororo Munroe is the daughter of an American photojournalist and an African princess. After her parents are tragically killed in an explosion in Cairo, Egypt, the toddler grows up on the streets, becoming a very skilled thief and pickpocket. Early in her teens, the self-possessed Ororo leaves the city, drawn by an irresistible urge to walk towards the far-distant mountains of Kenya.

At her journey's end, she becomes a protector to the region's impoverished tribes, using her recently developed mutant power to manipulate weather to ease the harshness of her worshipers' lives. This idyllic existence comes to an abrupt end when telepath Charles Xavier convinces Ororo to use her gifts to benefit all mankind as one of his X-Men.

> *"Here's where I belong... every nerve connected with the **wind**, the **clouds**, the **vapor**."*
>
> ORORO

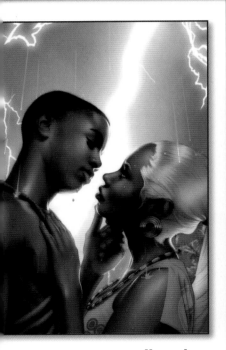

Young love
While trekking from Egypt to Central Africa, Ororo meets the young T'Challa as he undertakes the Wakandan manhood rite: a walkabout ordeal. When the prince is attacked by South African mercenaries, Ororo's newly manifesting powers save them both, and a romance develops. Eventually, duty pulls them apart and they go their separate ways. T'Challa returns to Wakanda, while the young mutant continues towards her destiny in Kenya.

Uniform is composed of unstable molecules: invisible and intangible until activated by Storm's lightning power.

African queen
Overcoming initial suspicion, Ororo champions the cause of mutants in Wakanda. However, when old enemy Shadow King takes over the minds of T'Challa and X-Men leader Cyclops, Storm is hunted by her own teammates and new subjects. As a favored adopted daughter of the Panther God, Bast, Ororo receives divine help to overthrow the domination of the psionic puppet master and free her people.

Storm's mohawk is a highly visible sign of her rebellious streak.

DATA FILE

REAL NAME: Ororo Munroe (briefly Ororo Iqadi T'Challa and Ororo Komo Wakandas)

FIRST APPEARANCE: *Giant Size X-Men* (Vol. 1) #1 (May 1975)

OCCUPATION: Adventurer, educator, mutant and human rights activist, former Queen-Consort of Wakanda

AFFILIATIONS: X-Men, Avengers, Fantastic Four, Panther God, Jean Grey School

POWERS/ABILITIES: Weather control and generation; expert fighter; skilled thief and pickpocket

BASE: New York City; mobile

End of the affair

When the X-Men and Avengers go to war over mutant messiah Hope Summers, the clash results in Wakanda being drowned by a Phoenix-force empowered Sub-Mariner. As Storm sides with the X-Men, she loses the support of the Wakandans, and her marriage to T'Challa is annulled after a bitter fight with him. Although separated, Ororo remains deeply devoted to T'Challa and his people.

RAINING QUEEN

Mutant Super Hero and Earth-born goddess to the world's poor and underprivileged, Ororo Munroe is a true force of nature. A forthright and inspirational leader, she guides her teammates into combat as effectively as she commands the elemental forces of the planet. Her indomitable willpower allows her to overcome crippling claustrophobia and makes her one of the most formidable fighters ever to defend Earth.

CIVIL WAR

Following the outbreak of superhuman civil war in the U.S., T'Challa and Ororo consult powerful non-aligned nations and rogue states. They aim to quell fears that Black Panther, his mutant bride, and Wakanda may pose a destabilizing threat to the fragile balance of world affairs.

Black Panther (Vol. 4) #20 (Nov. 2006) *Diplomatic negotiations quickly sour when Inhuman king Black Bolt realizes his own people despise the 'primitive' humans T'Challa and Storm.*

OVER THE MOON

The growing U.S. crisis prompts the Inhumans to invite Wakanda's royal couple to a diplomatic meeting in Attilan on the moon. It is a trip that further exhibits T'Challa's technological advances. However, the Inhumans' request that he intervene in a dispute over Terrigen crystals stolen by the U.S. ends in acrimony when the African heroes learn that many Inhumans still use genetically created slave labor.

TEST OF METTLE

After an idyllic honeymoon, newlyweds T'Challa and Ororo pay a courtesy call to Latveria. When they reject Doctor Doom's overtures to form an alliance against the American superhumans currently squabbling with each other, Doom tries to kill his guests. T'Challa reveals his inventive genius with his own version of Doom's armor and the resultant battle wrecks Latveria's power grid, allowing the royal couple to escape.

BETWEEN THE DEVIL AND THE DEEP

When Reed Richards asks T'Challa to join the pro-registration side of the civil war, the royal couple visit Atlantis. Namor cordially relates how he fought beside T'Challa's grandfather, Azzuri. He then implores them to lead international resistance to the Superhuman Registration Act and the superhuman army the U.S. is believed to be covertly building to attack other nations with superhuman inhabitants. With a heavy heart, the Black Panther agrees.

Black Panther (Vol. 4) #21 (Dec. 2006) *Following discussions with Namor, Black Panther knows he must confront injustice wherever it appears.*

Black Panther (Vol. 4) #19 (Oct. 2006)
Doom utterly underestimates the power of his potential political hostages.

> *"When **you** were in caves, we were charting the stars."*
> BLACK PANTHER

Black Panther (Vol. 4) #22 (Jan. 2007) *When Stark's crude political ploy fails, T'Challa and Ororo teach him that his mechanical enforcers are useless against them.*

Black Panther (Vol. 4) #25 (Apr. 2007) *Despite his initial desire to remain neutral, T'Challa eventually realizes he must stand beside those heroes opposing the Registration Act.*

AMERICAN NIGHTMARE

After meeting initial resistance in Britain, T'Challa and Ororo finally visit the U.S. Under martial law, Washington D.C. is a hotbed of protest. When Tony Stark tries to force Storm to publicly register despite her diplomatic immunity, a riot erupts and the government deploys giant robotic Sentinels. Soon the situation deteriorates into a deadly battle and a full-scale diplomatic incident.

Black Panther (Vol. 4) #25 (Apr. 2007) *T'Challa reveals to Ororo that as Captain America has surrendered, he accepts the responsibility of leadership.*

CHOOSING SIDES

The civil war escalates when anti-registration hero Goliath is killed. Unable to remain impartial, the Black Panther joins Captain America's side fighting against the Act. He agrees to spearhead a mission to penetrate the illegal prison for superhumans his former friends Tony Stark and Reed Richards are operating in the Negative Zone. Before he can act, however, T'Challa learns that Cap has surrendered, leaving him in charge.

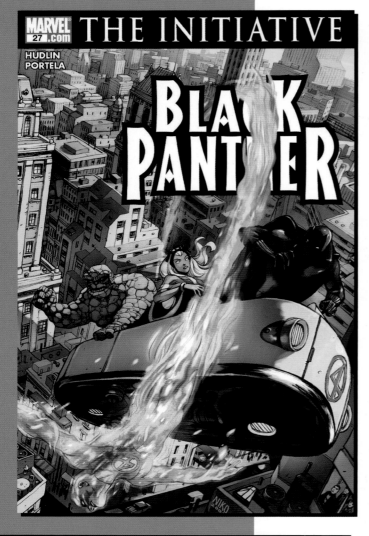

MARVEL.com 27
THE INITIATIVE
HUDLIN • PORTELA
BLACK PANTHER

JUNE 2007

BLACK PANTHER (VOL. 4) #27

THE NEW FANTASTIC FOUR ARE TRAPPED IN A ZOMBIVERSE WHERE THEY'RE ON THE MENU!

When the Wakandan Embassy in New York City is destroyed, newlyweds T'Challa and Ororo move into the Baxter Building and temporarily replace Reed and Susan Richards in the Fantastic Four. Following one epic mission, the new team comes home for a little peace and quiet, but is immediately plunged into another incredible crisis.

MAIN CHARACTERS
New Fantastic Four (Black Panther, Storm, Thing, Human Torch)

SUPPORTING CHARACTERS
Shuri • *Dora Milaje* • G'Mal

MAIN LOCATIONS
Baxter Building, New York City • Wakanda • Prison 42, Negative Zone • Skrullworld

1 Within hours of returning to the Baxter Building, T'Challa and Storm's downtime is disturbed by a giant wood-eating bug that has escaped from the Negative Zone. Although the creature is not hostile (just very hungry), its destructive rampage is something that even the Royal Guards and *Dora Milaje* cannot cope with.

2 The monstrous bug is immune to the team's powers and looks certain to escape into the outside world. With their options limited, T'Challa hunts for a suitable deterrent in Mister Fantastic's laboratory. There, he learns that the bug is not alone, but just one of thousands of creatures that have come through a portal linking Earth to S.H.I.E.L.D.'s other-dimensional Prison 42.

3 Ignoring all other distractions, the Black Panther returns to the fray. However, he soon discovers that even Reed Richards' formidable armory has nothing that can effectively handle the increasingly belligerent and apparently insatiable bug. Moreover, the starving creature is about to break out of the building and attack an unsuspecting city outside.

4 With no scientific solution able to stop the insectoid, the Black Panther reluctantly employs the mystical time-warping King Solomon's Frog in an attempt to exile the creature from Earth. Unfortunately, while trying to get closer to the bug, the four heroes are caught in the frog's aura when the unstable device prematurely activates.

5 In a flash of light, the team and the insect invader are catapulted across universes to materialize high above an alien planet. Storm catches T'Challa and the Torch lands safely thanks to his blazing powers. However, the Thing plummets down and smashes—painfully, but without harm— into the futuristic city below.

"An unstoppable bug and Skrulls. Could things get worse?"

BLACK PANTHER

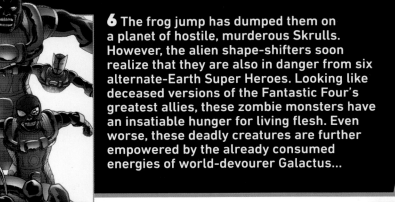

6 The frog jump has dumped them on a planet of hostile, murderous Skrulls. However, the alien shape-shifters soon realize that they are also in danger from six alternate-Earth Super Heroes. Looking like deceased versions of the Fantastic Four's greatest allies, these zombie monsters have an insatiable hunger for living flesh. Even worse, these deadly creatures are further empowered by the already consumed energies of world-devourer Galactus...

DOCTOR DOOM

Doctor Doom is the ultimate despot, whose power and genius confirms his conviction that he is the rightful ruler of all he surveys. His uniquely inventive mind, sorcerous expertise, tactical brilliance, and sheer ruthlessness make Doom the most dangerous man in existence.

The Great Destroyer

Learning of the imminent destruction of the multiverse at the instigation of the Beyonders, Doom uses time travel technology to place himself at the beginning of the crisis. As Rabum Alal—the Great Destroyer—he devises a cult of super-beings dubbed Black Swans. These devotees cautiously counteract the Beyonders' forces, while subtly setting in motion Doom's own grand scheme to survive and conquer all that remains after reality ends.

Doom's royal regalia conceals both mechanical and magical weapons and defenses.

Doom constantly modifies his armor to keep one step ahead of his many enemies.

> "I am Doom...Destroyer of worlds...What gods dare stand against me?"
>
> VICTOR VON DOOM

ORIGIN

Born of a Romani healer and a witch who sold her soul to Mephisto, Victor von Doom is raised by his clan, and proves to be an outstanding inventor. Accepting a scholarship to New York State University, he clashes with Reed Richards, his only intellectual equal. Misusing college resources, von Doom builds an inter-dimensional engine to breach Hell and save his mother, but he impatiently rushes his calculations.

When the machine explodes, scarring him forever, Victor journeys to Tibet where mystic monks forge a metal mask and armor to hide his shame forever. Years later, he resurfaces as monarch of his homeland Latveria to begin war with the Fantastic Four and other Super Heroes.

DATA FILE

REAL NAME: Victor von Doom

FIRST APPEARANCE: *Fantastic Four* (Vol. 1) #5 (Jul. 1962)

OCCUPATION: King, conqueror

AFFILIATIONS: Zefiro Romani clan, Sub-Mariner, Black Swans

POWERS/ABILITIES: Brilliant scientist and sorcerer

BASE: Castle Doom, Doomstadt, Latveria; Battleworld

MORLUN

Morlun roams the multiverse devouring beings enhanced by gods and spirits. His insatiable hunger for totem-energy and the power it provides makes him practically unbeatable. Manifested in Wakanda by the Crocodile Cult of Sobek to destroy the dominant Panther God's avatars, the pitiless Morlun turns on his summoners. He also consumes the Jabari Man-Ape, before targeting newly ordained Black Panther, Shuri. Meanwhile, T'Challa and Queen Ororo are fighting to escape the Realm of Death. They succeed by drawing in Morlun to challenge Death Incarnate, and escaping back to the living world while the deadly entities clash.

ERICH PAINE

Genoshan geneticist Erich Paine sets up his laboratory of horrors in Niganda, Africa, creating mutant monsters to threaten the entire region, including Wakanda.

A mercenary creating beasts for unsavory clients, Dr. Paine's venture is sponsored by Erik Killmonger and aided by Ivan Kragoff, the Red Ghost. However, the gene splicer's ultimate goal is duplicating mutant super-powers in his own body. His atrocities are ended when T'Challa leads a team of X-Men deep into Niganda to battle and defeat legions of scientifically altered creatures. With his dreams thwarted, Red Ghost executes Paine, and Kragoff's Super-Apes use the research for their own ends.

THE CANNIBAL

The Cannibal is an invisible energy-based parasitic force that possesses and absorbs its hosts, transferring from one body to another by a kiss. Once it vacates a body, the host immediately dies. After being commissioned by Klaw to disrupt and sabotage Wakandan diplomacy in the U.S.—and murder T'Challa—the Cannibal takes over the body of T'Shan, Wakandan Ambassador to the U.N.

T'SHAN

Son of previous Black Panther S'Yan, T'Shan resents his cousin T'Challa for years after being defeated by him in the ritual combat to chose the king. Grudgingly accepting the situation, T'Shan serves Wakanda as an international diplomat. When possessed by the Cannibal, T'Shan seems a willing participant, working secretly with the parasite to destroy T'Challa. He and the energy force both vanish and are presumed killed during the Skrull invasion of Wakanda.

HOMELAND INVADERS

Some of T'Challa's most insidious enemies have attacked him in the very heart of his homeland. For some menaces, even Wakanda's highly secure borders provide no barrier.

SECRET INVASION

When their Throneworld dies, religious frenzy grips the Skrulls and they begin a wholesale infiltration of Earth, intent on making it the new heart of their star-spanning empire. Soon the entire planet is infested with their agents—even impregnable, unconquered Wakanda.

*"How **much trouble** could one **little African nation** really be?"* Commander K'vvvr

SEE WAKANDA AND DIE

As a Skrull battle fleet approaches Wakanda, its arrogant Commander K'vvvr expects his undetectable shape-shifting fifth column to have destroyed every trace of potential resistance. At the border, however, K'vvvr and his crew are shocked when they see a killing field strewn with the bodies of their advance guard—Wakanda's traditional warning to all invaders throughout its history.

Black Panther (Vol. 4) #39 (Sep. 2008) *The horrified Skrulls cannot conceive how the primitive humans have penetrated their supposedly infallible disguises.*

FACE THE ENEMY

An inconclusive clash of high-tech hardware and skilful electronic hacking quickly deprives both sides of advanced weaponry and power. Although the Wakandans bring the alien warships crashing to Earth, it is at the cost of their own computerized systems. This war will be settled in the way of ancient warriors, through physical combat.

Black Panther (Vol. 4) #39 (Sep. 2008)
The pride of the Skrull starfleet humiliatingly smashes to Earth.

Black Panther (Vol. 4) #40 (Oct. 2008) *Once again, the Skrulls triumph by masquerading as a hero's most trusted companion.*

MASTERS OF WAR

With no other option, two proud races meet on the battlefield, fighting hand-to-hand in the manner of their ancestors. Although all Wakandans don sacred Panther attire to battle fiercely for their homeland, two undercover Skrulls seemingly seize the initiative by ambushing and capturing Queen Ororo and King T'Challa.

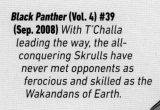

Black Panther (Vol. 4) #39 (Sep. 2008) *With T'Challa leading the way, the all-conquering Skrulls have never met opponents as ferocious and skilled as the Wakandans of Earth.*

Black Panther (Vol. 4) #41 (Nov. 2008) *At long last, the Black Panther and Storm have the Skrulls exactly where they want them...*

A CUNNING PLAN

The Black Panther's scheme to destroy the invaders involves elaborate subterfuge. T'Challa leaves two Skrull infiltrators apparently undetected and, with the battle hanging in the balance, lets these sleeper agents capture him and Ororo, and bring them aboard K'vvvr's ship. Then, after secretly switching places with their Skrull tormentors, they kill the commander and lead their army of Panthers to victory.

MESSAGE RECEIVED

After ruthlessly exterminating every Skrull soldier, T'Challa's victorious forces cram a partially functioning spaceship with corpses and send it back to the Skrull leadership. The message is one every Black Panther has sent to any force foolish enough to challenge the might of Wakanda and the power of the Panther God.

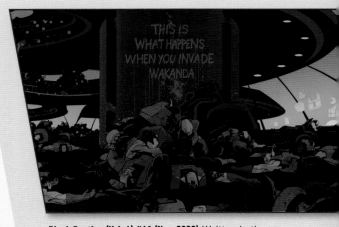

Black Panther (Vol. 4) #41 (Nov. 2008) *Written in the blood of the fallen, Wakanda's age-old answer to invaders never fails to make its point.*

Doomwar (Vol. 1) #4 (Jul. 2010)
After Doctor Doom plunders Wakanda's Vibranium reserves, Queen Shuri leads a Super Hero army against the tyrant's upgraded Doombots. Her fearless example proves beyond doubt she is a true Black Panther and a worthy warrior queen of the Wakandan people.

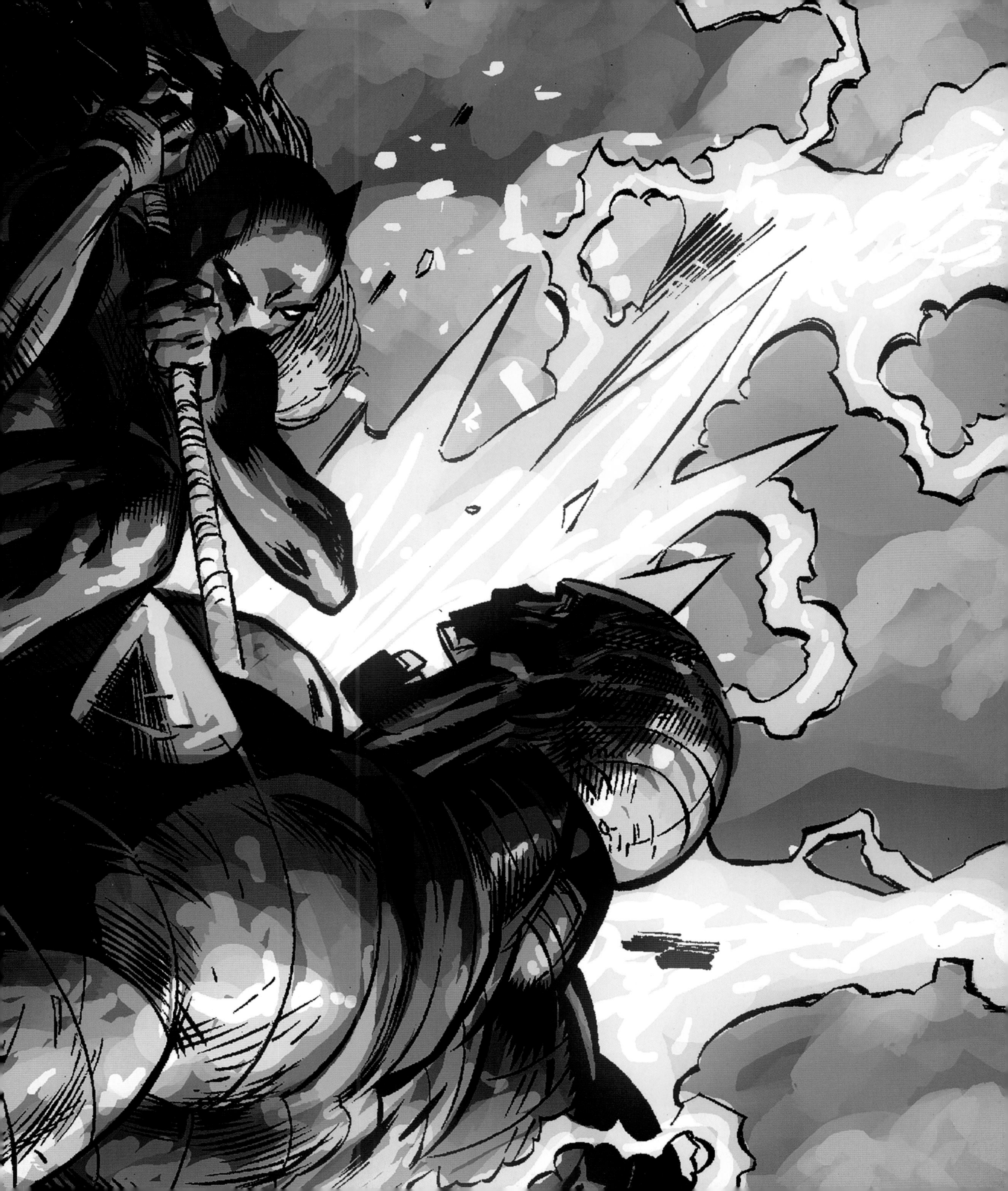

DOOMWAR

Doctor Doom secretly backs the radical Wakandan isolationists, the Desturi, while manipulating Queen-Regent Shuri, T'Challa, and the Fantastic Four into battling the Sub-Mariner. With all his enemies distracted, the Master of Latveria makes his move.

Doomwar (Vol. 1) #2 (May 2010) *Despite all his efforts, T'Challa arrives too late to preserve his nation's legacy.*

LEADERS-IN-EXILE

With Shuri and T'Challa away, Desturi extremists stage a lightning coup in Wakanda and imprison Storm. She is promptly put on trial—charged with treason, witchcraft, and crimes against humanity. Unable to help her, Shuri and T'Challa seek allies among the U.S.'s Super Heroes. Although officially neutral in political affairs, Storm's X-Men comrades volunteer to join a rescue mission.

Doomwar (Vol. 1) #1 (Apr. 2010) *T'Challa is greatly relieved when he sees the X-Men assembled ready to rescue his wife and win back Wakanda.*

VIBRANIUM HEIST

The crisis has been orchestrated by Doctor Doom in a Machiavellian move to seize Wakanda's processed Vibranium. The despot knows that the miracle mineral will greatly increase his magical power and has wrecked Wakanda simply so that he can plunder the national vault of all 10,000 tons stored there.

COUNTERSTRIKE

The liberators' retaliation is rapid and devastatingly effective. In one night, the country is freed thanks to the efforts of the X-Men, the Panthers, and the latter's elite *Dora Milaje* bodyguards. With the Desturi High Council eradicated, the nation is saved, but Doom has already achieved his aims and now has the means to become omnipotent.

Doomwar (Vol. 1) #2 (May 2010) *When T'Challa and Shuri return to the royal palace, their vengeance is swift and remorseless.*

Doomwar (Vol. 1) #4 (Jun. 2010) *Righteous fury fuels Shuri's ferocity in destroying the V-Series Doombots.*

THIS MEANS WAR

By the time T'Challa and Reed Richards find him, Doom has constructed an army of Vibranium-augmented war machines. Refusing to quit, Earth's heroes target Doom's numerous factories to destroy the robots, while Deadpool is hired to steal the tyrant's funds. The battle turns in the heroes' favor, but too late, as Doom dons magically enhanced Vibranium armor and readies himself to vanquish Earth with his sorcery.

"Wakanda is ours! Wakanda for Wakandans!"

DESTURI ONE

Doomwar (Vol. 1) #6 (Oct. 2010) *A defeated Doctor Doom bows before the harsh judgment of a true monarch, Queen Shuri.*

REGENT'S REVENGE

To stop Doom, T'Challa turns the villain's own magic against him, using alchemy and quantum science to neutralize all the processed Vibranium on Earth. This drastic act shatters the magician's plans, but also destroys Wakanda's economy and wealth in one stroke. Shuri then delivers her sentence of retribution: Doom must now live with the shame of failure and in fear of future Wakandan reprisals.

Doomwar (Vol. 1) #3 (Jun. 2010) *Doctor Doom considers himself the master of every situation. He is seldom proved wrong.*

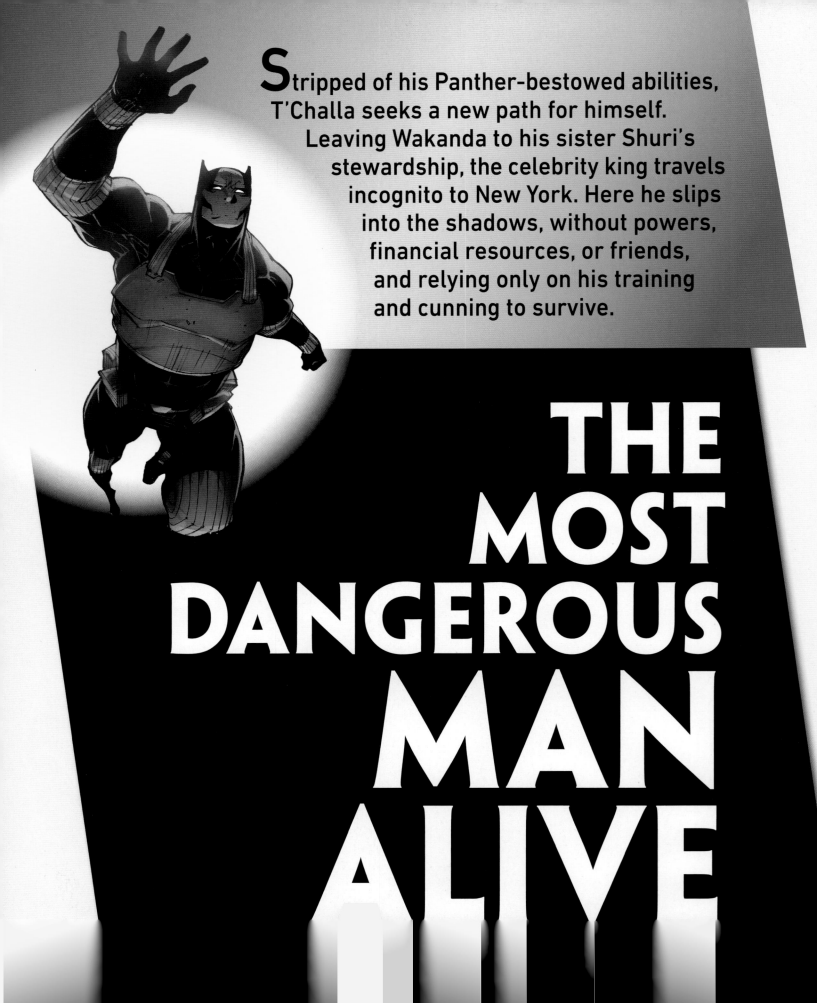

Stripped of his Panther-bestowed abilities, T'Challa seeks a new path for himself. Leaving Wakanda to his sister Shuri's stewardship, the celebrity king travels incognito to New York. Here he slips into the shadows, without powers, financial resources, or friends, and relying only on his training and cunning to survive.

THE MOST DANGEROUS MAN ALIVE

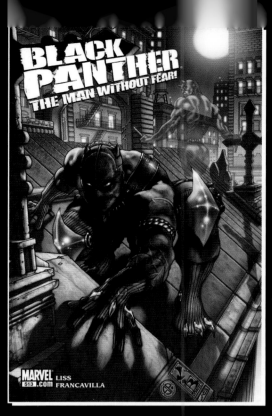

Black Panther (Vol. 1) #513 (Feb. 2011)
The Panther becomes a lone vigilante, safeguarding the mean streets of Hell's Kitchen in Daredevil's absence.

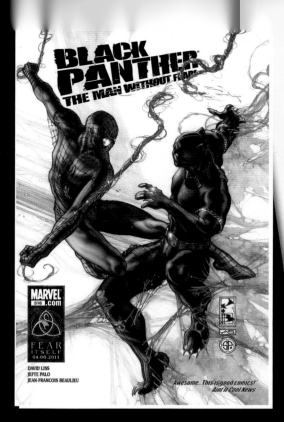

Black Panther (Vol. 1) #516 (May 2011)
Former Avenger ally Spider-Man offers T'Challa his help and won't take no for an answer!

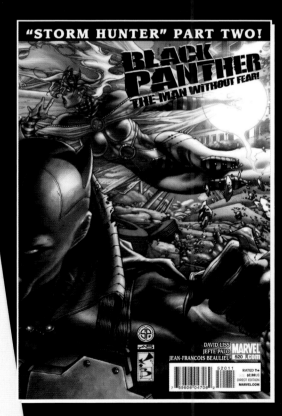

Black Panther (Vol. 1) #520 (Aug. 2011)
A clash with Kraven leads to an unexpected reunion with the Queen of Wakanda.

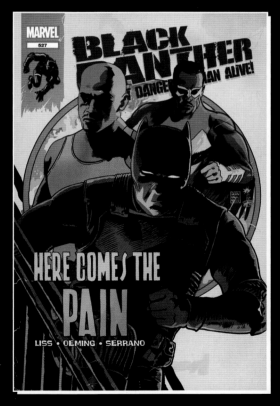

Black Panther (Vol. 1) #527 (Feb. 2012)
With a trusted team of allies at his side, the Panther battles the Kingpin with the fate of Wakanda at stake.

BLACK PANTHER:
MOST DANGEROUS MAN ALIVE!
(VOL. 1) #524

WITH NEW YORK OVERRUN BY SPIDER-POWERED RIOTERS, T'CHALLA LEAPS INTO ACTION!

When the Jackal unleashes a bioengineered plague in Manhattan, thousands of victims gain amazing arachnid characteristics. As the city's heroes battle the chaos and seek a cure, T'Challa's newfound abilities save lives and uncover a deadly plot—hatched by Hell's Kitchen's greatest menace—that threatens Wakanda.

DECEMBER 2011

MAIN CHARACTERS
Black Panther (T'Challa)

SUPPORTING CHARACTERS
Overdrive • Kingpin/Wilson Fisk • Lady Bullseye • The Hand

MAIN LOCATIONS
Shadowland Citadel • Hell's Kitchen, New York City

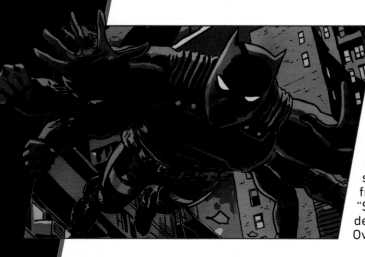

1 As thousands of eight-limbed freaks rampage across New York, T'Challa adapts quickly to his altered state while chasing Overdrive, a car-manipulating mercenary in the employ of Kingpin. After narrowly saving a pregnant woman from a horrific death, "Spider-Panther" becomes determined to stop Overdrive at all costs.

CRASH!!

2 The frantic pursuit endangers everyone on the streets and ends with Overdrive smashing into the Shadowland Fortress and stealing a "package" crucial to the Kingpin. Before the hero can react, the fast and furious criminal transporter drives off again...

3 Renewing the chase through streets and alleys, T'Challa eventually forces Overdrive to spin out of control. However, before he can apprehend the mercenary and claim the stolen prize, they are both ambushed by Kingpin's chief assassin, Lady Bullseye.

4 Lady Bullseye has also been mutated by the spider plague and is more formidable than ever. As she battles T'Challa to a standstill, Overdrive sees his chance to escape and roars off in his modified sports car.

> *"At least let me get the virus. **Spider** me up. How long does this take **anyhow**?"*
>
> OVERDRIVE

5 With Black Panther and Lady Bullseye relentlessly tracking him, escape proves impossible for Overdrive. As T'Challa finally gains the upper hand and disposes of Lady Bullseye, Overdrive is forced to concede defeat, allowing T'Challa to liberate his "cargo."

6 The much sought-after package turns out to be a young girl whose financier father oversees mergers and acquisitions on Wall Street. She explains to the Panther that the Kingpin had kidnapped her to force her dad to secretly buy up land in some place called "Wakanda."

FEAR ITSELF

A long-imprisoned Asgardian deity, the Serpent, awakens to unleash global terror and death. Its impact resonates throughout New York City's Hell's Kitchen, where, deprived of the Panther Spirit's powers, T'Challa battles a wave of prejudice and hate ravaging his adopted home.

HAMMER TIME

As the Serpent's many mystic hammers smash to Earth, one snags an orbiting spiritual fragment of the villain Hate-Monger. It carries the malignant essence to New York City, where it merges with disaffected, ineffectual bigot Josh Glenn. Utilizing newfound powers of persuasion, Glenn instigates a wave of racist atrocities in the multicultural community of Hell's Kitchen.

Black Panther: The Man Without Fear **(Vol. 1) #521 (Sep. 2011)** *Hate-Monger's essence is caught in the Serpent's magical mallet as it plunges towards New York.*

Black Panther: The Man Without Fear **(Vol. 1) #521 (Sep. 2011)** *T'Challa, as Mr. Okonkwo, sees the American Panther has taken sacred religious regalia and twisted it into something hateful.*

FLAMES OF HATE

As the new Hate-Monger, Glenn incites mobs of citizens to attack foreigners such as Sofija and recent African immigrant Mr. Okonkwo, secretly T'Challa in disguise. When Okonkwo tries to resist, he is checked by the American Panther, a dark, twisted counterpart to T'Challa's former heroic self.

HOSTAGE SITUATION

As Hate-Monger's influence grows, he takes over the local police precinct. Previously arrested for being an illegal immigrant, T'Challa is ready to liberate the precinct from Hate-Monger's grip. Battling his supremacist counterpart, American Panther, to a standstill, T'Challa incapacitates the mind-controlled police force and prepares for a final showdown.

Black Panther: The Man Without Fear **(Vol. 1) #522 (Oct. 2011)** *Mind-controlled cops and American Panther are no match for T'Challa's fury.*

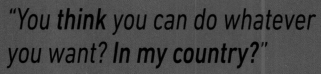

> *"You think you can do whatever you want? In my country?"*
>
> AMERICAN PANTHER

Black Panther: The Man Without Fear (Vol. 1) #523 (Nov. 2011) The terror subsides as soon as T'Challa removes the Hate-Monger's malign influence.

Black Panther: The Man Without Fear (Vol. 1) #523 (Nov. 2011) With Hate-Monger warping minds in Hell's Kitchen, T'Challa fights to save the purity of the sacred Panther's image.

MAGIC GOES AWAY

T'Challa and Sofija confront the possessed demagogue at a huge rally. When American Panther leads an all-out attack, T'Challa uses a hastily constructed jamming device to expel Hate-Monger's spirit from Glenn's body. Deprived of his master's mystical powers to influence emotions, American Panther is quickly defeated and thrown to the baying mob.

NEVER-ENDING HATE

Without his mind-controlling abilities, Josh Glenn is easily subdued and arrested. Elsewhere, the American Panther's costume goes missing, but is soon seen on a new, anonymous tormentor preparing to continue the racist crusade of exclusion and persecution...

Black Panther: The Man Without Fear (Vol. 1) #523 (Nov. 2011) The crisis may be over, but the flames of hatred still burn in some souls.

FOES
WITHOUT PITY

Deprived of the Panther God's blessing, T'Challa searches for purpose and confirmation of his worth by defending Hell's Kitchen for his absent friend Daredevil. He soon learns that a true hero is defined by the ferocity of his enemies.

HATE-MONGER

After being fired for his racist views, office worker and conspiracy theorist Josh Glenn becomes a paranoid demagogue stirring up attacks on immigrants.

When the Panther stops him stealing guns, Glenn's emotional turmoil attracts the spiritual energy of the original Hate-Monger. It possesses the bigot's body, granting him powers of spellbinding oratory and psychic persuasion. As the new Hate-Monger, Glenn creates an aura of intoxicating rage that sparks riots in the streets. He also recruits a powerful and symbolic accomplice—the American Panther—to aid his supremacist agenda. Seizing control of a police station, Glenn is finally subdued and arrested when T'Challa builds a device that can cancel out the villain's powers by banishing Hate-Monger's essence.

VLAD THE IMPALER

As a child, Vladimir Dinu was part of Romania's super-soldier project, developing matter-to-energy conversion powers. Able to energize objects, he hides this fact from his masters and, as an adult, moves to the U.S. Slowly making his way up the criminal hierarchy in New York City, Vlad eases himself into position as overlord of Hell's Kitchen, after the fall of the Kingpin and his successor the Hood.

Believing himself untouchable, Vlad's dreams of creating a powerful dynasty are methodically dismantled by T'Challa. Moreover, Vlad's precious anonymity is destroyed in an escalating public war with the "Man Without Fear," which culminates in a fierce street battle and the mastermind's downfall.

DR. HOLMAN

A figure of mystery with many clandestine resources and contacts, maverick biologist Dr. Holman insinuates herself into the local hospital and creates a secret lab of mutagenic horrors. Selling her monsters to the highest bidder, she soon comes to the Panther's attention, but her empire starts to crumble after she agrees to develop super-powers for Nicolae Dinu, son of Vlad the Impaler. Although she fails with Nicolae, Holman's process empowers the criminal's half-brother Gabe and kidnap victim Brian Fitzgerald. However, they escape before she can exploit them. She then attempts to end T'Challa's interference by tricking Kraven the Hunter into killing him, but the ploy backfires and they take her down together.

AMERICAN PANTHER

When his American father's murderer escapes punishment in a foreign court on a technicality, the victim's son becomes obsessed with revenge and develops a twisted sense of patriotism. Blaming all foreigners for the travesty of justice his father received, he joins the New York police force, abusing his position to attack immigrants. Singled out by Hate-Monger Josh Glenn, the corrupt cop is molded into a potent symbol of intolerance, prowling Hell's Kitchen at night as the American Panther.

The masked, unnamed villain rides a wave of bigotry and discontent incited by the Hate-Monger, savagely and publicly attacking foreigners, until T'Challa depowers and defeats Glenn, and then takes down the American Panther. Both villains are subsequently arrested for their crimes.

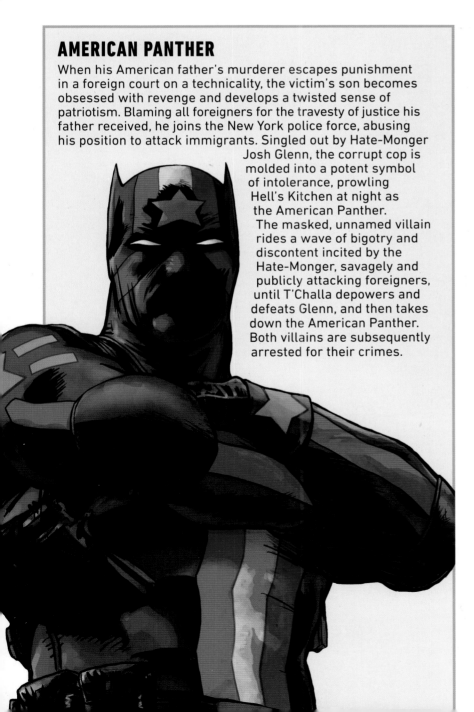

NICOLAE DINU

Ambitious Nicolae Dinu—son of Vlad the Impaler—shares his father's lust for wealth and power, but not his patience, strategic skills, or super-powers. While supposedly working for Vlad, Nicolae makes every attempt to undermine his father by botching many of Vlad's operations. Nicolae also secretly sponsors Dr. Holman's experiments to give him superhuman abilities greater than that of his father's.

Ruthless and brutal, his attempts to kill the vigilante Black Panther go badly awry, with T'Challa punishing the would-be usurper. Vlad is then forced to show his son how "real men" deal with such problems...by eliminating Nicolae and taking charge himself.

MAN WITHOUT FEAR

To redeem his honor and reevaluate his life's purpose, T'Challa relocates to Hell's Kitchen in New York City, replacing Daredevil as its guardian. Stripped of his powers, the Panther pits his ingenuity and training against an insidious, seemingly untouchable enemy...

Black Panther: The Man Without Fear (Vol. 1) #514 (Mar. 2011) Checking up on his friend, Cage cannot accept T'Challa's need to prove himself is worth risking lives.

URBAN JUNGLE

Between running a Hell's Kitchen diner as Mr. Okonkwo and cleaning up petty criminals as the Panther vigilante, T'Challa keeps busy. Soon his activities comes to the attention of superhuman Romanian mob boss Vlad the Impaler. Pervasive, powerful, and brutally effective, the gang lord prefers working behind the scenes rather than draw the unwelcome attention of police or meddling Super Heroes.

Black Panther: The Man Without Fear (Vol. 1) #514 (Mar. 2011) The new vigilante in Hell's Kitchen wants it clearly understood that he will not tolerate criminals.

POWER GRAB

When old ally Luke Cage insists on helping, T'Challa endangers their friendship by refusing. Meanwhile, Nicolae hires mad scientist Dr. Sheri Holman to give him his father's powers, but her own monster-making experiments also bring Holman to T'Challa's attention. Growing increasingly unstable, Vlad takes the war to his enemy in spectacular battles that light up Hell's Kitchen and allow Sofija to deduce that her boss is the Panther vigilante.

FAMILY BUSINESS

Vlad's eldest son, Nicolae Dinu, plans to supplant his super-powered father, but his inept handling of the vigilante's attacks force the Impaler to come out of the shadows and take personal charge. As his war against the mob intensifies, T'Challa is similarly distracted when his new waitress—enigmatic, military-trained Sofija—points out that a serial killer is quietly working in the neighborhood.

Black Panther: The Man Without Fear (Vol. 1) #513 (Feb. 2011) Vlad soon realizes that his inept older son Nico is no match for the new vigilante wrecking the Dinu family's criminal enterprises.

> "My pride, honor, and determination... these things are not bound to a crown, or position."
>
> T'CHALLA

Black Panther: The Man Without Fear (Vol. 1) #515 (Apr. 2011) Vlad sacrifices his entire family just to face the vigilante who has shattered his plans.

Black Panther: The Man Without Fear (Vol. 1) #513 (Feb. 2011) T'Challa shrewdly uses his enemy's own ambushes as a way to draw his prey closer.

DEATH MATCH

When the serial killer shoots Vlad's wife Angela, T'Challa arrives on the scene and is mistaken by the Impaler as her murderer. The Romanian's steely reserve finally shatters and he begins a self-destructive vendetta that brings carnage to the streets and ultimately costs him everything, even the loyalty of his adored younger son, Gabe.

CLASH OF EGOS

With the vigilante's identity revealed, Vlad invades the Devil's Kitchen diner and attacks everyone. Still looking out for his friend, Luke Cage intervenes to save the customers, leaving T'Challa to settle scores with a now completely deranged Vlad, who kills his son Nicolae just to get to the Panther. However, the crime lord's downfall is swift, not even allowing Vlad the glory of a grand death; only humiliating public exposure and arrest.

Black Panther: The Man Without Fear (Vol. 1) #518 (Jul. 2011) Vlad the Impaler's empire ends with defeat and ignominious arrest.

We are family

After becoming an Avenger, Luke Cage and his girlfriend Jessica Jones have a baby. Both are superhuman private detectives and Cage constantly risks his life working with the Avengers. Eventually, Jessica gives in to his persistent marriage proposals. In a taste of things to come, the ceremony is nearly ruined when the wedding party is delayed by a rampaging A.I.M. Adaptoid.

ORIGIN

Framed for drug dealing, Carl Lucas is sent to the brutal Seagate Prison where he volunteers for unsanctioned cellular regeneration experiments. When cruel prison guards sabotage the process, the convict gains incredible strength and muscle density, which he uses to break out of jail. Returning to New York City, the fugitive takes the name Luke Cage and becomes a Hero for Hire, while working to clear his name. Cage finally succeeds after meeting millionaire martial arts Super Hero Iron Fist, and the unlikely pair become crime-busting partners.

A solid, no-nonsense problem-solver, Cage has his heart firmly set on helping people. He alternates between leading a street-level version of the Avengers and running his own private investigation and personal security company.

> *"The war is over when we **say** it's over."*
>
> LUKE CAGE

Cage's fists can bend metal and punch through buildings.

Hero for hire

When T'Challa begins his search for a queen, he visits a New York nightclub where a pop star flirts with him. After saving him from being shot by the pop star's jealous boyfriend, Cage becomes T'Challa's wingman and advisor. Their subsequent adventures together pit the mismatched heroes against criminal masterminds, ninjas, vampires, and many women keen to become T'Challa's wife.

LUKE CAGE

Strong, smart, and resolute, Luke Cage has experienced both sides of the justice system. The former street-gang member is always ready to fight for the little guy with a raw deal, and respond harshly to villains bent on hurting others.

STREET JUSTICE

Luke Cage is one of the toughest men alive and deals with every problem head on. Brash and confrontational, he prefers friends and foes to think of him as rash, impetuous, and not very bright. However, in truth he is a cunning and calculating warrior, determined to defend the weak and punish the wicked. He is also a fiercely protective family man who will do anything for his loved ones.

Steel-hard skin allows Cage to fend off bullets and even bombs.

Enhanced musculature increases Cage's speed, reflexes, and resilience.

DATA FILE

REAL NAME: Formerly Carl Lucas, legally changed to Luke Cage

FIRST APPEARANCE: *Luke Cage, Hero for Hire* (Vol. 1) #1 (Jun. 1972)

OCCUPATION: Adventurer, private detective, bodyguard

AFFILIATIONS: Heroes for Hire, Avengers, Defenders, Fantastic Four

POWERS/ABILITIES: Enhanced strength and durability, steel-hard skin

BASE: New York City

Friendly warning

When T'Challa, deprived of his Bast Panther powers, relocates to Hell's Kitchen as a vigilante, Cage repeatedly intervenes, concerned that his friend and role-model is out of control and out of his depth. Tired of being patronized and second-guessed, T'Challa finally snaps and uses martial arts to temporarily paralyze Cage and teach him a very public, and humiliating, lesson.

KITCHEN CREW

Shaken by recent setbacks—losing his throne, powers, and the blessing of the Panther God—T'Challa needs to prove he can make his way alone. Such a man attracts enemies as easily as allies...especially in New York's Hell's Kitchen, whose denizens can become either, or both.

"Can you understand wanting to start over? I think perhaps you can."

SOFIJA

KRAVEN THE HUNTER

Sergei Kravinoff has been both hero and villain in his long and eventful life: battling beside Nick Fury, but later against Ka-Zar, Daredevil, Tigra, and others. After years obsessively stalking Spider-Man, Kraven commits suicide, but is called back from the grave and trapped on Earth against his will. Deprived of joy or peace, he now pursues honor above all and is asked to repay a debt from his previous life to former acquaintance Dr. Holman, who wants him to kill the Black Panther. After an epic clash, T'Challa and Storm finally convince Kraven that Holman is a monster who experiments on animals, and he joins them in capturing her. Kraven then dedicates himself to rehabilitating her creations in the free wilderness of the Savage Land.

BRIAN FITZGERALD

Inoffensive Brian Fitzgerald works in the Devil's Kitchen run by Mr. Okonkwo—T'Challa in disguise—and is kidnapped in an attempt to draw out the vigilante Man Without Fear. Injured in the incident, Brian is exposed to Vlad the Impaler's power and is experimented on by rogue geneticist Dr. Holman. Brian gains Earth-shaping powers at the cost of his free will, and Holman uses his blood to create a serum imparting these same powers to Vlad's second son, Gabe.

Abducted by Gabe, the now brain-damaged and suggestible Brian becomes a pawn in the war between the Panther and Vlad.

SOFIJA

A veteran of Balkan conflicts with a wide and formidable set of skills, the mysterious Sofija applies for a waitressing job at the Devil's Kitchen. With her experience, she soon deduces her boss is the Panther vigilante waging war on organized crime all over town. Clearly accustomed to action and intrigue, Sofija quickly becomes a crucial information-gathering source and investigator for T'Challa. She identifies Iris as Hell's Kitchen's avenging serial killer and helps T'Challa finally defeat his adopted brother, Hunter. After the Dinu clan's fall, Sofija operates as Black Panther's back-up: a deadly sniper stationed outside Shadowland to ensure the Kingpin does not survive if his ninjas defeat T'Challa and his allies.

N.Y.P.D. DETECTIVE ALEX KURTZ

World-weary police detective Alex Kurtz spends the majority of his time investigating Matt Murdock's connection to Daredevil. However, when both disappear, the aging cop is forced to bring down crime lord Vlad Dinu.

Kurtz initially turns a blind eye to the activities of Hell's Kitchen's new masked guardian, but soon begins quietly helping the Black Panther. Kurtz is the first to realize that a serial killer is using Vlad's activities as cover for the killing of violent spouses and parents. Under-resourced and frustrated by the red tape hampering his job, Alex shares the information with T'Challa, trusting him to take action.

FRANKLIN "FOGGY" NELSON

Daredevil's best friend and confidant is Franklin Nelson. As Matt Murdock's partner, gentle, shy Foggy is privy to all the blind hero's secrets. When the disgraced champion leaves New York City to find himself, he asks former District Attorney Foggy to create fake immigration documents for T'Challa.

Already disbarred, Nelson risks federal imprisonment for creating an identity that would allow the former king of Wakanda to become humble diner manager "Mr. Okonkwo," recently emigrated from the Democratic Republic of Congo. As the Panther's war against Vlad the Impaler intensifies, Foggy is arrested, but T'Challa breaks into the F.B.I. and deletes Nelson's file, defending his brave comrade the only way he can.

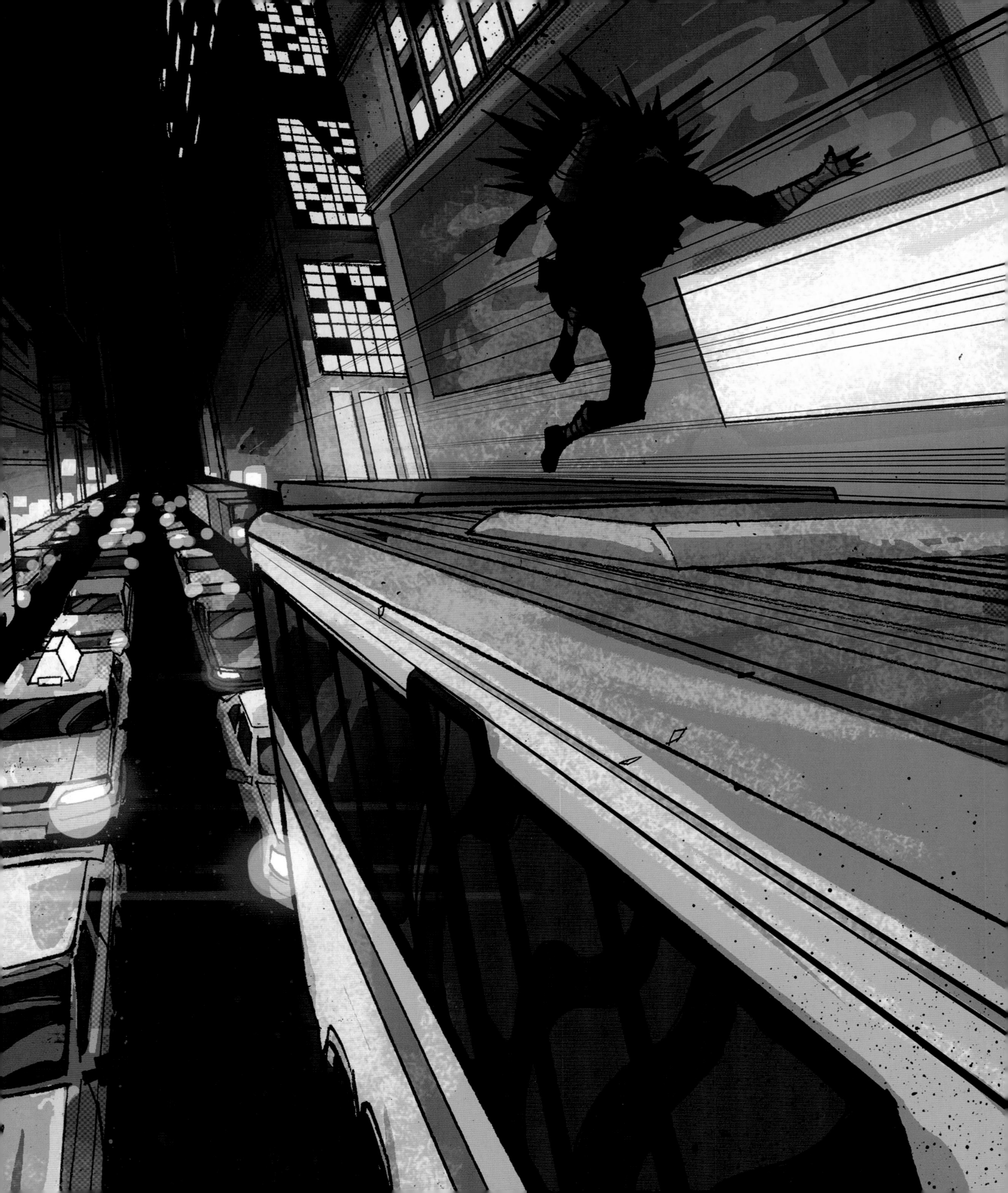

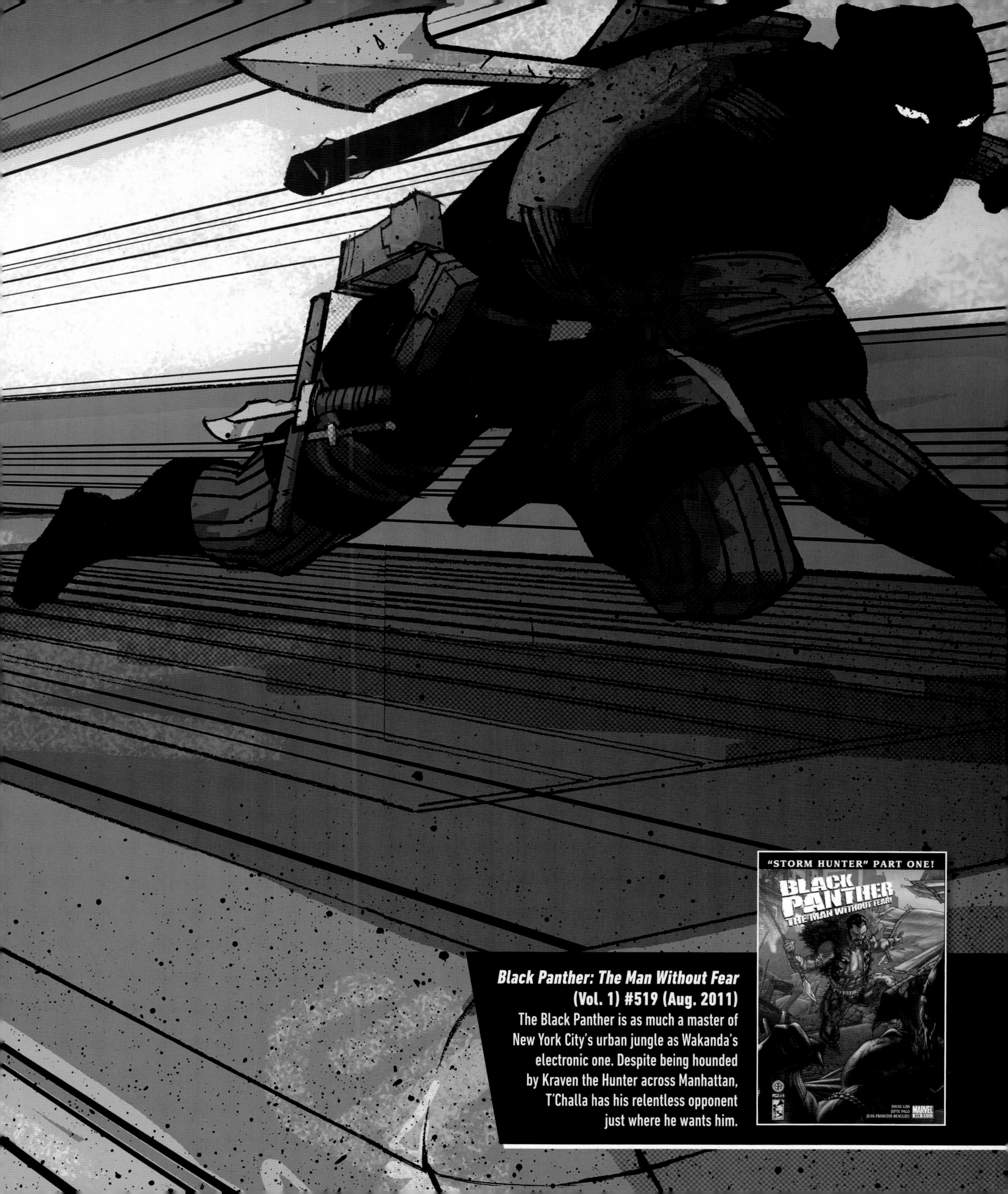
"STORM HUNTER" PART ONE!
BLACK PANTHER
THE MAN WITHOUT FEAR!
MARVEL

***Black Panther: The Man Without Fear* (Vol. 1) #519 (Aug. 2011)**
The Black Panther is as much a master of New York City's urban jungle as Wakanda's electronic one. Despite being hounded by Kraven the Hunter across Manhattan, T'Challa has his relentless opponent just where he wants him.

Poor but determined Wilson Fisk educates himself with stolen books and obsessively molds himself into a weapon through extreme bodybuilding and extensive martial arts training. After serving as a mobster's bodyguard, Fisk kills his boss and takes over. He smashes his way to the head of New York City's underworld by embracing brutally traditional methods as well as new technologies, such as a laser beam disintegrator in his cane, to force rivals and enemies to join his criminal syndicate. Successfully thriving below the police's radar, Fisk's relentless rise is halted by numerous clashes with Super Heroes like Spider-Man, Captain America, Daredevil, and Black Panther. These highly public battles temporarily drive him into exile in Japan and Europe, but the Kingpin always returns.

Family feuds

Wilson Fisk's greatest joy—and greatest weakness—are his wife Vanessa and his son Richard. As the Schemer and the Rose, the neglected boy twice tries to kill the Kingpin and take over his organization, only to be foiled by his mother, who finally executes Richard to eliminate him as a threat to Fisk. Vanessa later dies after blackmailing Matt Murdock into defending an incarcerated Kingpin, to secure her husband's freedom so that he can die well in a manner of his own choosing.

> *"The underworld will now be run like a **business**...and the chairman of the board will be...**the Kingpin**."*
>
> **WILSON FISK**

Futures investment

During the second superhuman civil war, Fisk restores his preeminent position by employing Janus Jardeesh, a living smokescreen who can block the visions of the precognitive Inhuman, Ulysses. With heroes unable to discern his activities, Fisk rebuilds his shattered empire before being betrayed by Jardeesh. However, a fearsome display of punitive brutality soon has the Kingpin on the ascent once again.

THE KINGPIN

Through sheer determination, sustained effort, and ruthless enterprise, Wilson Fisk rises from poverty and obscurity to become one of the most dangerous criminals on Earth. Neither Super Heroes nor underworld rivals can withstand the power of the Kingpin for very long.

DATA FILE

REAL NAME: Wilson Fisk

FIRST APPEARANCE: *Amazing Spider-Man* (Vol. 1) #50 (Jul. 1967)

OCCUPATION: Crime boss, businessman

AFFILIATIONS: The Hand, Hydra, Emissaries of Evil, Fisk Industries

POWERS/ABILITIES: Immense strength, trained martial artist, brilliant strategist

BASE: Mobile; formerly Fisk Tower, New York City; Westchester County; Las Vegas; Japan

King for a day

As leader of the ninja cult the Hand, Fisk takes over Wakanda's banking system to gain control of the country's land rights and exploit its untapped natural resources of oil, natural gas, and precious metals. While temporarily protecting Hell's Kitchen, T'Challa, Wakanda's king, uncovers the scheme and, with help from his sister Shuri, Luke Cage and the Falcon, ruins Fisk's plan.

THE BIG BOSS

Despite projecting an image of ponderous size, immense physical power, and unlimited resources, the Kingpin's greatest assets are simple: a razor-sharp mind, meticulous attention to detail, and a willingness to get his huge hands dirty when necessary. Although his wealth and studies have created a veneer of sophistication, at heart Wilson Fisk is a brutal killer who will do anything to achieve his goals.

Fisk's sartorial elegance combines timeless style with concealed lethal weapons.

The Kingpin's huge bulk masks an ability to move and react at lightning speed.

147

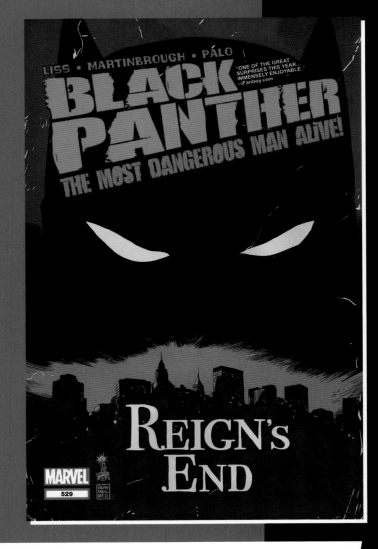

LISS • MARTINBROUGH • PÁLO

BLACK PANTHER
THE MOST DANGEROUS MAN ALIVE!

"ONE OF THE GREAT SURPRISES THIS YEAR... IMMENSELY ENJOYABLE."
—iFanboy.com

REIGN'S END

MARVEL
529

APRIL 2012

MAIN CHARACTERS
Black Panther (T'Challa)

SUPPORTING CHARACTERS
Luke Cage • The Falcon • Kingpin (Wilson Fisk) • Black Panther (Shuri) • Sofija • Lady Bullseye • Typhoid Mary

MAIN LOCATIONS
Shadowland Citadel • Hell's Kitchen, New York City

BLACK PANTHER:
MOST DANGEROUS MAN ALIVE!
(VOL. 1) #529
AS THE PANTHER BATTLES THE KINGPIN, WAKANDA'S FUTURE IS AT STAKE.

Abdicating his throne, T'Challa safeguards New York's Hell's Kitchen in place of the missing Daredevil. Discovering that the crime lord Wilson Fisk, a.k.a. Kingpin, has used the ninja cult the Hand to cripple Wakanda's economy, the Black Panther strikes back.

1 With allies Luke Cage and the Falcon, T'Challa breaks into Kingpin's Shadowland Citadel, where they are met by an army of Hand assassins. The ninja defenders have no idea that the raid is merely a ruse to distract their enemy, or that T'Challa's secret weapon, Sofija, is stationed outside with a sniper rifle in case the heroes fail.

2 Ever cautious, Kingpin orders his trusted servant Miyu to secure the Hand's financial database. The files, which were used to infiltrate Wakanda's banks and treasury to buy up thousands of acres of the mineral-rich country, also contain all Fisk's records. Ordering his elite assassins Lady Bullseye and Typhoid Mary to handle Black Panther's comrades, Kingpin decides to face T'Challa himself.

3 In the computer room, Miyu uses Fisk's codes to stabilize Wakanda's economy and plants a worm to send details of the Hand's illegal activities to global enforcement agencies. When Fisk's acolytes discover this betrayal they attack. Miyu kills them all and reveals herself to be T'Challa's sister, Queen Shuri, who had earlier taken the real Miyu captive.

*"Now Panther...
we **end** this."*

4 As Cage and Falcon battle Lady Bullseye and Typhoid Mary, Shuri dons her own ceremonial Black Panther suit and joins the battle. The tide is quickly turned and the trio rush to T'Challa's side, fearing that he may be outmatched by the titanic Kingpin.

5 In a furious duel, T'Challa battles Kingpin to a standstill while strategically and psychologically outmaneuvering him. The worm in the Hand's databanks has left Fisk enough money and secrets to rebuild, but should he try to retaliate, it will destroy all his files, bankrupting his organization. The Black Panther has beaten Kingpin at his own dirty money game.

6 Having proved himself in his own eyes, T'Challa meets with recently returned Matt Murdock and returns responsibility for safeguarding Hell's Kitchen to Daredevil. Bolstered by a renewed sense of purpose and confidence, the Black Panther returns to his beloved Wakanda.

DATA FILE

REAL NAME: Samuel Thomas Wilson

FIRST APPEARANCE: *Captain America* (Vol. 1) #117 (Sep. 1969)

OCCUPATION: Adventurer, hero, trainer, S.H.I.E.L.D. agent, social worker

AFFILIATIONS: Avengers, Invaders, S.H.I.E.L.D. Super-Agents, Heroes for Hire

POWERS/ABILITIES: Peak-human strength, speed, reflexes and agility; powered flight; avian psychic link enables him to see through eyes of all birds

BASE: New York City; mobile

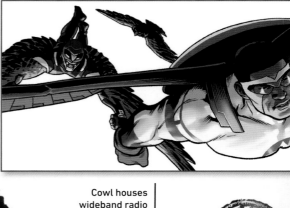

Cowl houses wideband radio equipment and vision-enhancing lenses.

FLIGHT AND FIGHT

Sam Wilson learns early how to face adversity. After losing both parents to gang crime, he leaves high school before graduation and educates himself. Drifting through life, he works as an artist, urban planner, and social worker. He learns falconry and how to fight before establishing himself as a powerful defender of the weak in both his civilian and costumed personas. He is afraid of nothing, possessing the self-confidence to face any crisis or menace head on.

Bird on a wire

From his early days as a two-fisted costumed acrobat to his high-flying time as an Avenger and agent of S.H.I.E.L.D., the Falcon travels all over the globe, but never forgets his roots as a champion of the inner city. Whether battling cheap crooks, Super Villains, robots, monsters, or even other Super Heroes, Sam Wilson remains at heart a man of the people.

Flight-suit is layered with Vibranium microweave strong enough to withstand small arms fire.

New sentinel

After years proving himself a true hero, Sam Wilson inherits the role of Captain America when Steve Rogers is incapacitated by old age. The new Sentinel of Liberty proves more than equal to the task, but also becomes a controversial patriotic symbol by taking a stand on many social issues. He takes on a Super Hero apprentice in teenaged human/bird/vampire mutate Joaquin Torres to help him in his cause.

ORIGIN

Troubled Harlem orphan Samuel Wilson is transformed by the Red Skull's Cosmic Cube into the perfect partner for Captain America in a devious bid to destroy the Star-Spangled Avenger. However, Sam overcomes the Skull's programming and becomes a Super Hero in his own right, firstly as a costumed acrobat and later—after meeting Black Panther—as a flying, armored crusader with a psychic link to birds, like his pet falcon, Redwing. T'Challa constantly supplies the Falcon with flight-suit upgrades, and they become trusted allies, working together many times. The Falcon's dedication to helping the most helpless make him well known within the crime-fighting community. When Steve Rogers surrenders the role of Captain America, Sam naturally succeeds him.

"My life's an open book."

SAM WILSON

Perfect partner

The Falcon is a driven and passionate righter of wrongs, but his most important gift is an ability to mesh with other heroes. Having teamed up with practically every hero in the U.S., Sam works best and most often with street-smart brawler Luke Cage and African King T'Challa. Other than Steve Rogers, these are the heroes he most trusts and admires.

Holographic hard-light wings are magnetically powered.

THE FALCON

Trained by Captain America, Sam Wilson constantly strives to combat his tragic early life by seeking to help others. From the streets to the sky, the fearless Falcon overcomes all adversity with daring, determination, and cutting-edge technology—making the world a safer, fairer place for all.

FROM THE SHADOWLAND

From Shadowland in Hell's Kitchen, Wilson Fisk, a.k.a. Kingpin, manipulates financial markets to take control of Wakanda and its resources. To handle all potential resistance, he employs an army of deadly ninjas and a select cadre of superhuman killers.

TYPHOID MARY

A mutant with Dissociative Identity Disorder, Mary Walker manifests different powers with each of her identities and exhibits a pathological hatred of men. As the Kingpin's hireling, she repeatedly battles Daredevil and other heroes like Spider-Man and Wolverine, constantly and uncontrollably switching from sadistic seductress to homicidal maniac. As Mutant Zero, Mary works briefly alongside the heroic Civil War collective the Initiative, but ultimately returns to her manic mercenary ways.

When Daredevil and Kingpin clash in Hell's Kitchen over control of the ninja cult, the Hand, as well as the occult fortress Shadowland, Fisk rehires Typhoid Mary as one of his enforcers. Although a lethal opponent, Mary is totally unprepared for the ruthless combat tactics used by T'Challa and his allies.

LADY BULLSEYE

Japanese lawyer Maki Matsumoto is kidnapped by the Yakuza clan, but escapes when freelance assassin Bullseye kills her captors. Although Bullseye is unaware he accidentally saved her, Maki becomes fixated on the villain, modelling herself on him as a martial artist killer-for-hire and adopting his name for her own.

Employed by Hand leader Hiroshi, Lady Bullseye targets Matt Murdock; psychologically destabilizing him and orchestrating his corruption and takeover of the Hand.

MIYU

When Wilson Fisk takes control of the Hand, he accepts the centuries-old system of administrative structure and staff that keeps the ninja clan operating so efficiently. To oversee the many strands of his evil empire, Fisk employs a personal handmaiden, Miyu. An enigmatic woman of indeterminate age who possesses considerable martial arts expertise, Miyu has been the loyal liaison between many Hand leaders and their ever faithful soldiers.

As his schemes progress, Fisk falls increasingly under Miyu's seductive sway. After she is abducted and impersonated by Black Panther Shuri, the Kingpin's composure and plans to conquer Wakanda quickly fall apart.

THE HAND

A ninja sect that flourished in Japan 800 years ago, the Hand's roots lie deep in prehistory, when its founding fathers, known only as "the Sickly Ones," began worshiping a demonic "Beast." The Hand's mystic knowledge has been down through generations, permeating the organization's role as spies and assassins-for-hire. Its overarching agenda of covert conquest aims to bring the Beast to Earth, an ambition guided by the Hand's lethal breakaway faction, Snakeroot.

While constantly clashing with hero teams such as the Avengers and X-Men, the Hand perpetually seeks powerful yet ultimately corruptible leaders to follow. This permits each commander to dictate policy as the grand plan comes closer to fruition. At one time or another, leaders such as Elektra, Daredevil, the Mandarin, and Wilson Fisk have all thought they could use the ninjas for their own ends, only to find the Hand controlling them.

With the Marvel multiverse dying and every Earth in peril, the Black Panther and a band of super-smart heroes—the Illuminati—act on behalf of all Earth's inhabitants. Inevitably, however, the horrific measures forced upon these former friends and allies tear the group apart.

THE END OF DAYS

***New Avengers* (Vol. 3) #7 (Aug. 2013)**
T'Challa and Namor clash, but suspend hostilities to join together to save the collapsing multiverse.

***Avengers* (Vol. 5) #39 (Feb. 2015)**
Steve Rogers' Mighty Avengers of S.H.I.E.L.D. are deployed to stop the world-wrecking Illuminati.

***New Avengers* (Vol. 3) #28 (Feb. 2015)**
The Illuminati's devastating secret weapon to contain the Avengers is exposed.

***Avengers* (Vol. 5) #43 (Jun. 2015)**
With all options exhausted, Earth's overwhelmed heroes prepare for imminent annihilation.

AVENGERS VS. X-MEN

With Shuri ruling Wakanda and T'Challa anointed King of the Dead, global tensions rise as the Avengers and X-Men battle for possession of the Mutant Messiah, Hope Summers. As the destined vessel of the cosmic Phoenix Force, Hope holds the key to mutant salvation and the survival of humanity...

DESPERATION

The conflict escalates into cataclysmic battles, with Hope eventually fleeing to the mystical, other-dimensional city K'un-Lun. Realizing that she must inevitably carry the burden of the Phoenix, the young mutant seeks spiritual guidance and training from mystic warriors Lei-Kung and Iron Fist to enable her to handle the transformation.

DELIBERATION

There are fewer than 200 mutants left on Earth when the Avengers learn that the omnipotent Phoenix Force is about to return. Aware that the destructive energy creature is drawn to Hope Summers, the nervous heroes decide to take her into protective custody, regardless of her fellow mutants' objections.

Avengers vs. X-Men (Vol. 1) #10 (Oct. 2012)
Hope's training ends when the Phoenix Force compels an increasingly unstable Cyclops to invade K'un-Lun looking for her.

Avengers vs. X-Men (Vol. 1) #2 (Jun. 2012)
The Avengers are ready to fight their oldest allies to keep Hope hidden from the Phoenix.

DESTRUCTION

Despite the Avengers' efforts, the Phoenix reaches Earth, but is prevented from merging with Hope. Instead, it possesses Cyclops, Namor, Colossus, Magik, and Emma Frost, who use its immeasurable power to make Earth a mutant paradise. However, the Phoenix Force ultimately hungers for a single host and turns the mutants against each other.

Avengers vs. X-Men (Vol. 1) #5 (Aug. 2012) *Unable to control Hope Summers, the Phoenix Force possesses five other mutants and allows their secret desires to transform the world.*

> "This is a **mutant** problem.
> **We'll** handle it."
>
> CYCLOPS

Avengers vs. X-Men (Vol. 1) #2 (Jun. 2012) The Avengers are powerless as the Phoenix Force grants its mutant hosts unlimited power at the expense of human feeling.

Avengers vs. X-Men (Vol. 1) #7 (Sep. 2012) After millennia of resolute resistance, Wakanda falls to a superior force— a Phoenix-Force empowered and enraged Prince Namor.

DEATH

With the Phoenix Force malignly influencing its hosts, mutant utopia becomes hell on Earth. Giving in to a long-held grudge against T'Challa, the Sub-Mariner decimates Wakanda with a huge tidal wave. The ensuing carnage makes a remorseless enemy of the Black Panther, who swears to one day take Namor's life.

DIVORCE

As the wider war rages, T'Challa and Ororo clash. He cannot forgive her siding with the mutants and Namor's subsequent attack on Wakanda to destroy the Avengers hiding there. Fighting to a bitter stalemate, T'Challa, as Chief of the Panther Cult, annuls their marriage for aiding an enemy of Wakanda.

Avengers vs. X-Men: Versus (Vol. 1) #5 (Oct. 2012) Among the conflict's greatest victims are heartbroken survivors T'Challa and Ororo.

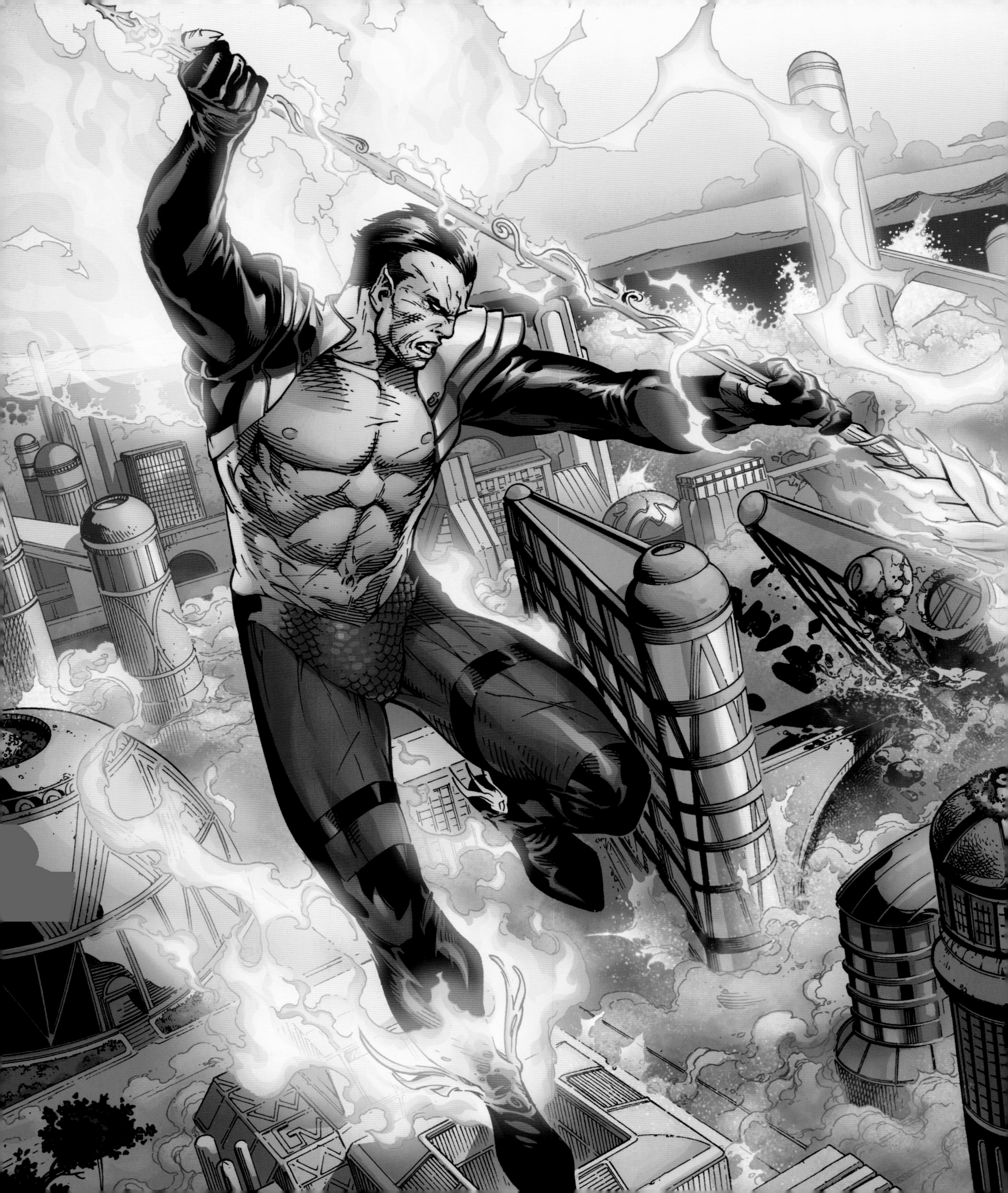

Avengers vs. X-Men (Vol. 1) #8 (Sep. 2012)
A devastating war between *Homo superior* and Super Heroes gives Marvel's first mutant an opportunity to settle old scores with the Black Panther. Namor's Phoenix Force-triggered tsunami decimates Wakanda, breaking T'Challa's heart.

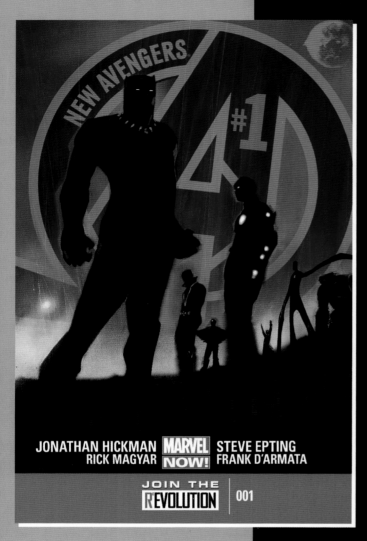

JONATHAN HICKMAN **MARVEL NOW!** STEVE EPTING
RICK MAGYAR FRANK D'ARMATA

JOIN THE **REVOLUTION** | 001

NEW AVENGERS (VOL. 3) #1

DENIED HIS POWERS AND THRONE, THE BLACK PANTHER LEARNS THAT ALL REALITY IS DOOMED!

Years earlier, T'Challa refuses to join the first gathering of the Illuminati. Now, as the Earth is threatened by overwhelming danger, the former king must abandon his principles and convene a new assembly of Earth's most brilliant heroes. The team faces tough choices if reality is to survive a series of catastrophic collisions between universes.

MARCH 2013

MAIN CHARACTERS
Black Panther (T'Challa)

SUPPORTING CHARACTERS
The Makers (N'Kono, Kimo, T'Dori) • Black Swan • Manifold • Illuminati (Captain America/ Steve Rogers, Reed Richards, Doctor Strange, Black Bolt, Tony Stark, Namor)

MAIN LOCATIONS
Necropolis of Wakanda (Earth-616) • Earth-1331

1 While participating in the Wakandan Makers' science ritual, teenagers N'Kono, Kimo, and T'Dori encounter a dimensional breach. As ruler of Necropolis—Wakanda's City of the Dead—T'Challa observes the situation unfold, and warns the students to stay back as he enters the rift. On the other side, Black Panther witnesses an alternate Earth about to smash into his world.

2 Operatives descend from the world above and the watching Wakandans learn that such planetary collisions are called "incursions," and their incidence is increasing. The invaders' leader—Black Swan—reveals that the only way to save any of the colliding Earths is to obliterate one of them. When T'Challa objects to such callous barbarity, Black Swan orders her men to open fire.

> *"Everything dies...*
> *It's inevitable...And I accept it."*
>
> REED RICHARDS

3 Their weaponry tears through Black Panther's defensive shields. He is unable to protect the young Makers and they are all killed. In a vengeful fury, Panther mercilessly attacks Black Swan's men as they prepare to destroy one of the encroaching Earths.

4 As T'Challa wades through her forces, Black Swan's deputy, Manifold, hesitates, unable to destroy an entire world. Black Swan summarily executes her disobedient subordinate and readies the trigger, dedicating the planet's destruction as a tribute to her master Rabum Alal, the Great Destroyer.

5 Black Panther pounces, but is too late to stop Black Swan detonating the device. Knocking her out, he can only watch in horror as the planet above is expunged and reality returns to normal around him. After praying to the Panther Spirit, Bast, T'Challa comes to a fateful decision.

6 Realizing he cannot save Earth and his universe alone, T'Challa calls former friends and allies he had previously abandoned. A new Illuminati resolutely unites to find a way to save everything in existence...

THE ILLUMINATI

Facing the eradication of all existence, T'Challa convenes the Illuminati. With elite thinkers drawn from all of the Earth's superhuman factions, he seeks to understand and stop the menace of colliding realities. The solution is unthinkable: to save their homeworld, the heroes must wipe out all other worlds and universes.

BEAST

Hank McCoy, a.k.a. Beast, is a highly principled theoretician, bringing both humanity and intellectual rigor to the debate. He inherits his position within the Illuminati from Charles Xavier and represents mutant kind. Having experienced great intolerance and seen his own species almost become extinct, McCoy agonizes over acts of extermination. However, he can find no solution to the crisis—even after heated disagreements with his own idealistic, time-displaced younger self.

SUB-MARINER

Fierce survivalist Prince Namor is the only Illuminati member prepared to accept the undeniable necessity of destroying other worlds to save their own. When the Illuminati is paralyzed over the ethics of the crisis, the Sub-Mariner unilaterally detonates an antimatter bomb to destroy an incursion from another Earth. When the group fractures, Namor assembles a new cabal of remorseless villains to help Earth survive further incursions.

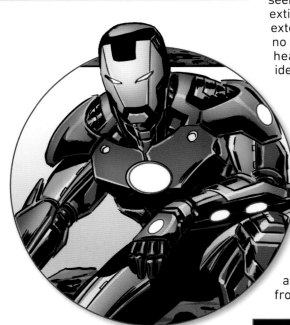

IRON MAN

Brilliant engineer Tony Stark never encountered a problem he couldn't solve. The arch-pragmatist believes he will always build some way to buck the odds. However, he falls victim to his own arrogant stubbornness after his technologies prove insufficient to handle the crisis and his morality prevents him from being a cold-hearted killer.

MISTER FANTASTIC

Probably the smartest man on Earth, Fantastic Four leader Reed Richards meticulously studies the problem of the colliding worlds and weighs all solutions against his own moral compass. Despite suggesting many countermeasures—all ultimately unsuccessful—Richards fatalistically accepts that in the end, "Everything dies."

BLACK BOLT

Blackagar Boltagon's slightest whisper can level mountains. Decades of isolation and self-imposed silence have accustomed the Inhumans' mute monarch to imperiously resolve problems. Black Bolt grows even more distant and unmanageable after becoming Celestial Messiah to the Kree. His solutions are not collaborative, but are carried out on his own initiative and solely for the benefit of his subjects.

DOCTOR STRANGE

Sorcerer Supreme Stephen Strange has experienced far greater and more mysterious realms than Earth. On finding that all existence is destined to fall, he abandons years of devotion to his own world. Without apology or consultation, and at the cost of his soul, Strange acquires godlike power to fight the threat from the malign forces he has spent his life combating.

HULK

Physicist Bruce Banner becomes the unstoppable Hulk whenever his emotional equilibrium is disturbed. He is called in after the Illuminati decide to stop the incursions by any means necessary. Banner, in control of his rampaging alter-ego, adds his scientific genius to finding a solution, while using Hulk's brute power to battle champions from the encroaching Earths, all determined to save their own universes.

CAPTAIN AMERICA

An unflagging and inspirational moralist, Steve Rogers refuses to sanction destroying innocent worlds to safeguard his own. Expelled from the Illuminati and mind-wiped by Doctor Strange, Rogers eventually recovers his memory to become an implacable opponent, resolving to stop his former comrades committing serial slaughter on a cosmic scale.

THANOS

An unwanted child, Thanos rebuilds himself and resolves to reshape the universe into a place that makes sense to him. Tragically, for all concerned, his twisted reasoning is that of a death-obsessed madman.

*"All life is **noise**. All life is **a distraction**. Therefore it has **no real value**..."*

THANOS

ORIGIN

Born on Saturn's moon Titan, Thanos is a mutant among the ancient colony of long-migrated Earthly Eternals living there. Afflicted with the Deviant Syndrome, his mother, Sui-San, tries to kill him on sight. The boy grows up lonely and disturbed, eventually leaving Titan for other worlds. He returns years later leading interstellar pirates to eradicate most of Titan's population. He next targets Earth, where Thanos seeks to make himself a god using a Cosmic Cube, but is foiled by Captain Mar-Vell and the Avengers.

Infatuated with the entity Mistress Death, Thanos attempts to wipe out all life or become a Supreme Being using artifacts of unimaginable power like the Infinity Gems. Following many failed ventures and repeated deaths, he returns as Avatar of Death and resumes his crusade of slaughter.

Suit is a personalized weapons-system with as much destructive firepower as an intergalactic battleship.

Courting death

Thanos is one of the greatest intellects in existence, but his powerful mind is twisted towards destruction and conquest. His heart also holds great love, but only for the Avatar of Death. Her continual rejections include frequently resurrecting Thanos and returning him to a life he utterly despises. And so he ceaselessly plots to subjugate or eradicate the universe around him, determined to remake an unsatisfactory existence into one he can control.

DATA FILE

FIRST APPEARANCE: *Iron Man* (Vol. 1) #55 (Feb. 1973)

OCCUPATION: World conqueror, mass-murderer, pirate

AFFILIATIONS: Black Order, Cabal, Zodiac, Infinity Watch

POWERS/ABILITIES: Super-strength, speed, senses; flight, invulnerability, telepathy, teleportation, energy generation, matter manipulation, and magic-wielding; bionic and cyber augmentation

CORVUS GLAIVE

Cruel Corvus Glaive revels in the destruction he wreaks as Thanos' second-in-command. While leading assaults on Earth, Corvus is killed by Avenger Hyperion. His atom-rending glaive-blade is stored in Wakanda's Necropolis and resurrects Corvus to join his wife Proxima Midnight and Thanos in Namor's Cabal. Surviving multiversal annihilation, he forms his own Black Order, but later perishes.

SUPERGIANT

Supergiant is a parasitic psychic omnipath whose powers make her mentally unhinged. After the Black Order occupy Wakanda, she enslaves Inhuman king Black Bolt, seizing the Illuminati's antimatter bombs intended to destroy alternate Earths during incursions. When the Illuminati attempt a rescue, she uses Black Bolt to defeat the heroes. Supergiant dies after activating one of the antimatter bombs, which is teleported to a distant planet by Maximus the Mad.

PROXIMA MIDNIGHT

Wife of Corvus Glaive and Thanos' most ardent acolyte, Proxima Midnight executes the Mad Titan's vicious orders with glee. She is with Thanos when they succumb to Thane's "Living Death," but is revived to join Sub-Mariner's Cabal. When the multiverse is reborn, she returns to Thanos, but repeated failures prompt him to abandon her. She is killed by the Asgardian death goddess Hela.

EBONY MAW

Although physically weak, Ebony Maw is a callous mind-pirate with irresistible powers of persuasion. Maw possesses Doctor Strange, using the sorcerer to find Thanos' son Thane and spy on the Illuminati. When Thane's powers finally manifest, Maw manipulates him into inflicting the "Living Death" on Thanos and Proxima Midnight, and strives to make Thane a greater menace than his father. He flees when this fails.

BLACK DWARF

Thanos orders devastatingly powerful, gleefully sadistic Black Dwarf to crush Wakanda, but his armies are decisively repulsed by indomitable Queen Shuri and her forces. As brother to Corvus Glaive and brother-in-law of Proxima Midnight, Black Dwarf receives unexpected mercy; his shameful defeat merely results in expulsion from the Black Order. Seeking redemption, he is killed by Kree enforcer Ronan the Accuser while defending orbiting Earth citadel the Peak from an Avengers counterattack.

BLACK ORDER

Thanos gathers a group of disciples to carry out his plans and absorb his destructive philosophies. These savage servants are his lethal emissaries of evil, but some harbor ambitions to be more than just deputies.

INFINITY

With reality fracturing, the Avengers head into space to intercept a vast alien fleet. Taking advantage of their absence, Mad Titan Thanos invades, seeking vengeance and the location of his own children, whom he has sworn to eradicate.

New Avengers (Vol. 3) #8 (Sep. 2013) *The dying multiverse is nothing to Namor compared to the slaughter of his subjects in Atlantis.*

FADE TO BLACK

When spies inform him that the Avengers are absent from Earth, Thanos invades. Deploying his Black Order to devastate the planet, the Mad Titan demands tribute from Black Bolt: the heads of all young Inhumans. This global catastrophe disrupts the Illuminati's efforts to stop extra-dimensional incursions destroying the multiverse; nevertheless, they begin organizing Earth's remaining superhuman defenders to save the world...

IMPERIUS WRECKS

Despite simmering animosity, Sub-Mariner and the Black Panther attempt to broker a truce between Wakanda and Atlantis. War has been brewing ever since Namor inundated T'Challa's Golden Kingdom while possessed by the Phoenix Force. Queen Shuri rejects their pleas, however, and attacks Atlantis with staggering force and chilling success.

Infinity (Vol. 1) #1 (Oct. 2013) *T'Challa and his allies reel as another crisis threatens the embattled Earth.*

ALL CHANGE

Thanos is killing all his children. As his lieutenants scour Earth for hidden progeny, they disguise their actions by seemingly seeking Power Gems from the Infinity Gauntlet. When Thanos confronts Black Bolt, the Inhuman king detonates a Terrigen bomb in the flying city of Attilan. This bathes the planet in transformative mists, activating the latent super-power gene of millions of Inhumans.

Infinity (Vol. 1) #3 (Nov. 2013) *Attilan's destruction above New York triggers the birth of many new Inhumans.*

"To protect a world, you must possess the power to destroy a world."

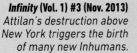
Captain Universe

New Avengers (Vol. 3) #9 (Oct. 2013)
Blockbusting Black Dwarf could not cope with a Black Panther defending his shattered homeland.

Infinity (Vol. 1) #6 (Jan. 2014) The Inhuman king, Black Bolt, has no defense against Supergiant's psychic domination.

ENEMY AT THE GATES

Black Order member Black Dwarf invades Wakanda, but is repulsed by T'Challa and Shuri's forces. Elsewhere, Proxima Midnight, also from Thanos' strike force, enters Atlantis—already decimated by Shuri's actions—to retrieve Namor's Infinity Gem. The heartsick Sub-Mariner soothes his seething rage by lying and telling the alien general what she seeks is hidden in Wakanda. This triggers the African nation's second alien invasion in days.

Infinity (Vol. 1) #6 (Jan. 2014) Thane proves Thanos is right to fear the power of his children by sealing him in amber.

MIND OVER ANTIMATTER

The Black Order finally occupies Wakanda and telepathic parasite Supergiant enslaves Black Bolt. She then takes possession of the Illuminati's arsenal of antimatter bombs, which are stored there to destroy alternate Earths during incursions. When the Illuminati mount a rescue, she turns Black Bolt on them, but is destroyed by cunning Maximus the Mad, who uses an antimatter bomb to destroy her.

FOREVER AMBER

As Thanos and the Black Order battle the Illuminati, the Avengers return from space and get the upper hand. Thanos' son Thane—beguiled by treacherous Ebony Maw—traps Thanos and Proxima Midnight in a "Living Death" of amber and flees Earth. With Thanos' threat ended, the Illuminati store him in Wakanda's Necropolis and focus on the greater menace of the incursions.

WHEN WORLDS COLLIDE

Black Panther's responsibilities escalate from defending Wakanda to preserving all reality. Additionally, his new Illuminati team starts to fracture in the face of truly overwhelming obstacles: a mysteriously self-destructing multiverse, and increasingly monstrous new foes.

SUB-MARINER'S CABAL

When the Illuminati proves unable to enforce its own resolution to destroy another Earth to save its own, Namor triggers the group's antimatter device taking full responsibility for the billions of deaths that follow. He then gathers villains and monsters to help preserve his own world at the cost of all others. His recruits—Thanos, Corvus Glaive, Proxima Midnight, Terrax, Maximus, and Black Swan— revel in savagery. However, after invading Wakanda and occupying Necropolis, they clash with the guilt-wracked Sub-Mariner when he criticizes their unnecessary carnage on the Earths they eliminate. When the Cabal betrays him, Namor leaves them to die during an incursion. However, the villains escape to an alternate Earth, where they build a life raft to survive the destruction of reality.

> *"Brothers, sisters...will you help me kill worlds?"*
> NAMOR

BLACK SWAN

Yabbat Ummon Turru survives her Earth's elimination by Black Priests. Rescued by the warrior-woman sect the Black Swans, Yabbat joins the sect in serving the Great Destroyer Rabum Alal (Doctor Doom). She is schooled in their ways and granted fantastic power.

Black Swans select and save one Earth in every incursion, but Yabbat is captured by the Black Panther when she arrives in Wakanda. Learning of the multiversal crisis, T'Challa asks the world's greatest minds to help him, forming the Illuminati. While a prisoner of the Illuminati, Yabbat informs them of the invading worlds, manipulating her captors and causing the team's breakup. She then joins Sub-Mariner's Cabal, resuming her mission to shatter worlds for the Great Destroyer.

THE BEYONDERS

The Ivory Kings, a.k.a. the Beyonders, are higher-dimensional entities from outside the multiverse who can create new realities—after first obliterating all current existence. The Beyonders target a multiverse for eradication, orchestrating the collision of alternate universes, with the Earth of each becoming the point of impact. When Doctor Doom learns of the Beyonders' plan, he uses time-travel to outwit and eliminate them, but his intervention is too late to save the multiverse. Taking the name Rabum Alal, Doom exploits the power he steals from the Beyonders to construct a Battleworld from fragments of the old multiverse. He then establish himself as the god of this new warring reality.

BLACK PRIESTS

Enigmatic and immensely powerful, Black Priests are a hive-mind collective of artificial beings who combine magic and science. Their role is to eliminate all Earths that become involved in an incursion, believing that by excising these planets, the remainder of each universe will survive.

The Black Priests ruthlessly crush all resistance on each Earth they encounter, but eventually come under the thrall of Doctor Strange. Quitting the Illuminati, Doctor Strange guides the Priests in completing their mission: to remove dying parts of the multiverse to save the greater whole.

MAPMAKERS

With Rabum Alal having stalled their scheme to obliterate the multiverse, the Beyonders create specialized servants out of A.I.M.-built Adaptoids that have become stranded between universes. These "Mapmakers" are tasked with charting and accelerating multiversal collapse.

Preceded by a biomechanical advance guard—the Sidera Maris—Mapmakers harvest Earths for anything of potential value, while also evaluating and neutralizing those worlds' ability to resist annihilation. They use incursions to reach their next target by crowding aboard a meteor-sized piece of a ravaged Earth and crashing it into another Earth, marking the latter as a future planetary victim for the Beyonders.

TIME RUNS OUT

All of creation is decaying. Parallel universes are collapsing and crashing into each other, while the Avengers and Illuminati turn on one another as failure greets their every effort to save reality. The end of everything is in sight...

New Avengers (Vol. 3) #28 (Feb. 2015) *Friends fight friends with no mercy and no chance of survival.*

THIS IS THE END

With extinction on the horizon for humanity, S.H.I.E.L.D. declares global martial law. Steve Rogers leads an Avengers team hunting the Illuminati. The Cabal of villains Sub-Mariner has recruited to eradicate incursion Earths runs amok, butchering the populations of each arriving world and reveling in the slaughter. When the Cabal occupy Wakanda, Black Panther Shuri dies battling them to allow her brother T'Challa to escape and carry on the fight.

New Avengers (Vol. 3) #24 (Nov. 2014) *Shuri battles valiantly for her brother, her nation, and her god.*

TRAITOR'S FATE

T'Challa's team, the Illuminati, still strive to find some way to save mankind with S.H.I.E.L.D. and Steve Rogers' Avengers fighting them all the way. Eventually, the ideologically opposed factions clash in a brutal battle that resolves nothing. The conflict ends with Invisible Woman revealing herself as Reed Richard's mole in S.H.I.E.L.D., allowing her teammates to escape once again. In the aftermath, Namor asks to rejoin the fugitive Illuminati.

RESTLESS SPIRITS

As King of the Dead, T'Challa is in constant communication with his father and all the other deceased Black Panthers. Even with existence ending, they only care about why T'Challa has not yet executed Namor for his unpardonable crimes against Wakanda.
T'Challa has his reasons. He is waiting for the moment Sub-Mariner is of no more use to him. Until then, the Panther will make him suffer...

The Avengers (Vol. 5) #40 (Mar. 2015) *T'Challa's Vibranium dagger pointedly reminds Namor the Black Panthers hold his life in their hands.*

> *"Other men do not make choices for me, Namor. Especially **not you**..."*
>
> BLACK PANTHER

The Avengers (Vol. 5) #40 (Mar. 2015) Expecting to be betrayed, supreme survivor Namor weathers Black Bolt's sonic assault and resolves to take his vengeance.

The Avengers (Vol. 5) #40 (Mar. 2015) Twisted monsters like Thanos welcome the end of all existence.

PANTHER'S REVENGE

Crushed by guilt, Namor conspires with the Illuminati to maroon the bloodthirsty Cabal on a world that is destined for antimatter extermination. Black Panther allows the plan to proceed, but at the decisive moment turns on Namor, having Black Bolt hurl him to his doom with Thanos and the rest of his former villainous allies. They have no idea that the indomitable Sub-Mariner will join an alternate, evil Reed Richards and escape destruction in a hastily constructed cosmic lifeboat.

REUNION

In the end, no solution works and the valiant heroes of the Illuminati at last acknowledge that nothing can save the multiverse. With reality ending, it's a time for final gestures. Some attempt to settle old grudges before it's too late. Others merely seek companionship, while a few regretful souls decide to make amends for mistakes and misdeeds that have burdened them for far too long.

New Avengers (Vol. 3) #23 (Oct. 2014) After years of fraught alliances, the Illuminati part company to perish separately.

DEFENSE OF THE REALM

Wakanda is perhaps the most well-armed and equipped country on Earth. Unconquered for 10,000 years, the warrior spirit of Wakanda can be seen in every weapon T'Challa has commissioned, designed, or built, and in the valiant reaction of his people whenever their beloved homeland is threatened.

TALON JET FIGHTERS

The Wakandan Design Group is a leader in aviation technology. It creates Talon jet fighters, helicopters, Quinjets, and stealth transporters such as sonar-gliders and magnetically powered aircars. Whether employed on military operations, relief work, or simple speedily efficient transportation, Wakandan aircraft are the envy of the world.

Black Panther (Vol. 6) #10 (Mar. 2017)

PROWLERS

Stationed throughout the land are Prowlers. These huge panther-shaped robotic weapons platforms are activated as a fail-safe response if Wakanda's borders are breached. As mobile weapons of last resort Prowlers are fully automated and programmed to carry out swift reprisals. Prone to being hacked, Prowlers have not been seen in recent years.

Hulk (Vol. 2) #33 (Dec. 2001)

N'YAMI BATTLE CRUISERS

Wakanda's greatest asset is a fleet of colossal flying aircraft carriers named in honor of T'Challa's birth mother. Although relatively slow-moving, N'Yami cruisers can operate in space and underwater. Each ship carries an energy cannon, projectile artillery, and Talon jet fighters.

Black Panther (Vol. 3) #33 (Aug. 2001)

FORCE MAJEURE

Wakanda celebrates an ancient culture of martial excellence to match its impressive developments in technology. Although the federation of tribes comprising the country are locally autonomous, the state of Wakanda maintains a small, well-trained military defense force. As current ruler, T'Challa prefers to use specialized units such as the *Dora Milaje* or *Hatut Zeraze* for undercover missions, surgical strikes, or other high-level operations. However, in times of nationwide crisis, every Wakandan—all touched in some way by the Panther Spirit—becomes part of a vast reserve ready to protect their country.

Black Panther (Vol. 3) #49 (Nov. 2002)

AFRIKAA

Young and idealistic Khairi Ngala is transformed by the mystic Heart of Africa into Afrikaa—an elemental lion-avatar tasked with saving Mohannda from exploitation and civil war. Afrikaa struggles in this mission until T'Challa and his ally Black Axe intervene, offering their advice, training, and expertise.

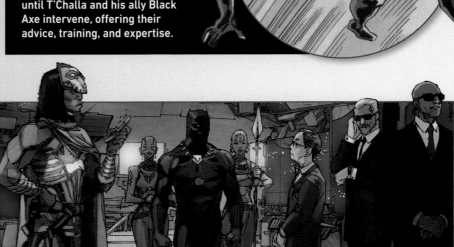

THE ULTIMATES

When T'Challa joins the cosmic preemptive-strike team the Ultimates, he staffs their Triskelion headquarters with his own Wakandan technicians and *Dora Milaje* warriors. He also puts a fleet of prototype spaceships, scanning systems, weapons, and vehicles at their disposal.

THE FALCON

After Captain America temporarily develops super-strength, T'Challa brings the Falcon—Cap's crime-busting partner Sam Wilson—to Wakanda. To complement the Falcon's acrobatic abilities, Sam's costume is equipped with solar powered, jet-propelled glider wings. The wings are also ultra-durable and electronically linked to Sam's brain. Subsequent upgrades deploy Wakandan holographic hard-light wings triggered by a cybernetic link. The Falcon's visor contains a suite of sensors, while lift and thrust are provided by minute magnetic drive engines housed in the back of the suit.

VIBRAXAS

In a lab accident, Wakandan teenager N'Kano gains uncontrollable vibration powers, making him a menace to himself and those around him. Vibraxas' abilities—creating shockwaves, sporadic frequency variation, and phasing through matter—are brought under control after T'Challa fashions a suit to regulate his energies and prevent his bones from shattering.

FANTASTIC FOUR

During Klaw's first attack on the Fantastic Four, the heroes find themselves helpless against their living-sound assailant. They are saved by a remote-controlled rocket from Wakanda that carries oscillation-absorbing Vibranium bands, allowing Mister Fantastic to touch and defeat Klaw.

FANTASTIC FORCE

Seeking to give Vibraxas purpose and turn his affliction into a boon, T'Challa sends the young hero to the U.S. to be trained by the Fantastic Four. When the legendary quartet suddenly disbands, the Black Panther founds, funds, and eventually leads a new team in their honor: Fantastic Force.

AVENGERS

When the Avengers battle Ultimate Ultron at the United Nations, the expanding Vibranium globe provided by T'Challa is used by Thor to contain the malevolent A.I.'s catastrophic self-destruction. Their courageous actions save New York City from total annihilation.

POWER PLAY

The Black Panther frequently uses his scientific genius and Wakanda's superior technological resources to bolster the capabilities of allies and comrades in their neverending fight against evil.

BLACK AXE

Black Axe is more than 15,000 years old, an immortal mercenary dedicated to the arts of war. Master of every combat discipline, he employs a high-tech axe and mechanized Vibranium armor. When he joins the Black Panther to save Mohannda from Cardinal Technologies, his arsenal of weapons is further upgraded by T'Challa.

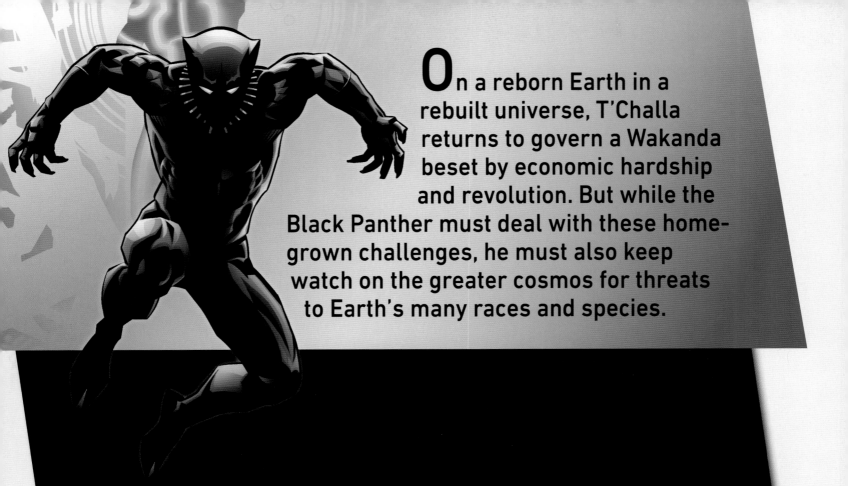

On a reborn Earth in a rebuilt universe, T'Challa returns to govern a Wakanda beset by economic hardship and revolution. But while the Black Panther must deal with these home-grown challenges, he must also keep watch on the greater cosmos for threats to Earth's many races and species.

ONCE AND FUTURE KING

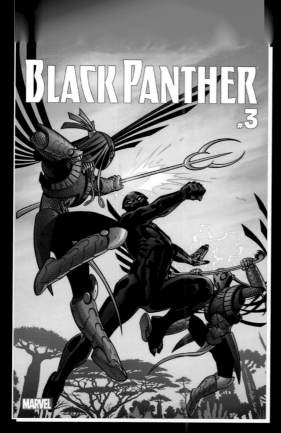

Black Panther (Vol. 6) #3 (Aug. 2016)
T'Challa faces violent dissent from those he trusts most—
rogue *Dora Milaje*, the Midnight Angels.

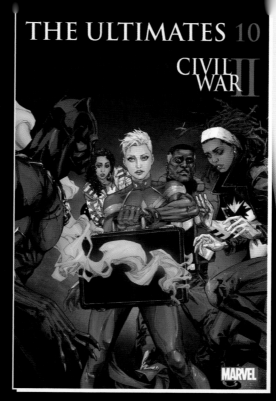

The Ultimates (Vol. 2) #10 (Oct. 2016)
The second superhuman civil war tears apart the
Ultimates, a squad of planetary saviors.

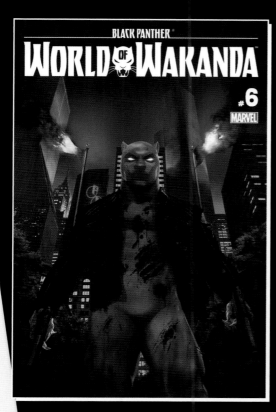

**Black Panther: World of Wakanda (Vol. 1) #6
(Jun. 2017)** The Panther's former disciple Kasper
Cole accepts one last mission as the White Tiger.

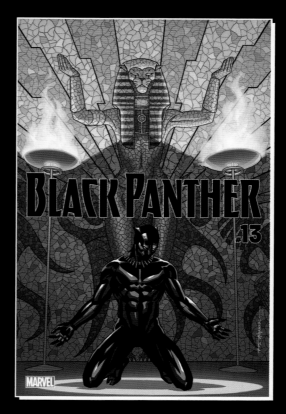

Black Panther (Vol. 6) #13 (Jun. 2017)
Wakanda is attacked by ancient devils and T'Challa
discovers their gods—the Orisha—have abandoned them!

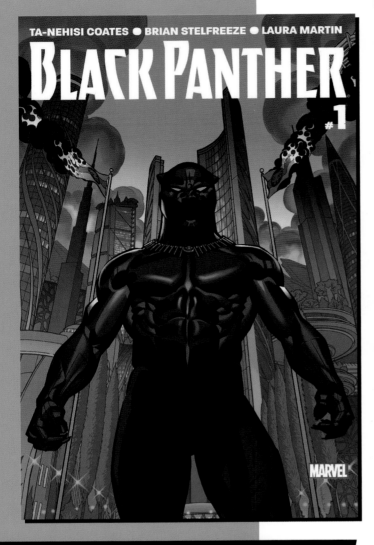

TA-NEHISI COATES ● BRIAN STELFREEZE ● LAURA MARTIN

BLACK PANTHER #1

MARVEL

JUNE 2016

MAIN CHARACTERS
Black Panther (T'Challa)

SUPPORTING CHARACTERS
Ramonda • *Dora Milaje* •
Midnight Angels (Aneka and Ayo)
• The People (Zenzi and Tetu)

MAIN LOCATIONS
The Great Mound • Birnin Zana
(Golden City) • Fort Hahn •
Necropolis • Nigandan Border
Region

BLACK PANTHER (VOL.6) #1

THE PANTHER FACES A REVOLT THREATENING TO DESTROY WAKANDA FROM WITHIN.

With Queen Shuri seemingly dead, T'Challa rules again. However, Wakanda is now a broken nation, struggling to recover from alien invasion, a devastating war with Atlantis, occupation, and economic collapse. As the returned king struggles to inspire his disillusioned people, a conspiracy of super-powered insurgents prepares to topple the ruling Panther Cult forever.

1 Wakanda's prosperity always depended on the Great Mound. However, when T'Challa visits disgruntled Vibranium miners in a bid to resolve their issues, an outside force psychically amplifies their anger. With tension mounting, the king's guards open fire on the unarmed workers.

2 The situation rapidly descends into a bloody riot. Meanwhile, in the midst of the clash, the Black Panther senses that some hidden enemy is directing the dissatisfaction of his people, manipulating events for their own ends.

3 In the Golden City, Queen Mother Ramonda adjudicates in the trial of a disgraced *Dora Milaje*, Aneka. The warrior captain is accused of overstepping her authority and punishing a local chieftain for taking slaves and abusing women in his village. Aneka is sentenced to death.

> *"It is **not enough to be the sword**, you must be **the intelligence behind it**."*
>
> QUEEN MOTHER RAMONDA

4 T'Challa's mysterious enemies are superhuman rebels Tetu and Zenzi. Safely concealed from detection, they rally rebel converts into the terrorist cell they call "the People." Encouraged by the success of their first strikes, they galvanize troops in the long-disputed Nigandan Border region for their next assault on Wakanda's stability.

5 Awaiting execution in Fort Hahn, Aneka is explosively broken out of prison by her lover, Ayo, using stolen Midnight Angel power suits. Aneka and Ayo go on the run, determined that they will live their own lives from now on, no matter the ultimate cost.

6 With chaos and dissent swirling around him, T'Challa returns to his laboratory in Necropolis. Here, Queen Shuri lies in a state between life and death, as she was left after Namor's Cabal invaded and occupied Wakanda. Desperate for trustworthy allies, the king prepares to finally resurrect Shuri and release her from "the Living Death."

A NATION UNDER OUR FEET

Devastated by successive attacks, the people of Wakanda are in despair. Rebel factions arise pursuing new political paths and different ways of living. Ancient traditions are discarded and, with his rule threatened, the Black Panther seeks a way to reconnect with his distraught, disenchanted people, or lose them—and Wakanda—forever.

POWER TO THE PEOPLE

As T'Challa strives to rebuild Wakanda, superhuman revolutionaries act to oust the ruling family. Secretly backed by foreign interests, the People, a terrorist cell led by empath Zenzi and elemental mage Tetu, incite violent confrontations to topple the Panther Clan and all it stands for. Their greatest early victory is almost killing Queen Mother Ramonda in a suicide bombing.

Black Panther (Vol. 6) #4 (Sep. 2016)
With bombs exploding in the streets, Zenzi's gift for emotional manipulation finds fertile ground in the anger and fear of war-torn Wakandans.

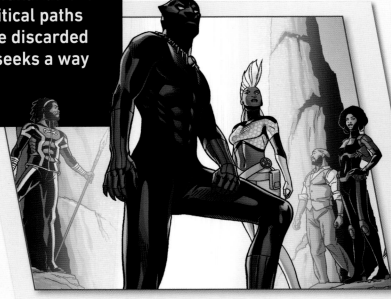

Black Panther (Vol. 6) #8 (Dec. 2016) *Manifold, Storm, Luke Cage, and Misty Knight, a.k.a. the Crew, are happy to help T'Challa take on the enemies of Wakanda.*

ANGELS OF MERCY

Dora Milaje mutineers Ayo and Aneka flee unjust condemnation using stolen war-suits. As vigilante renegades the Midnight Angels, they uncover wholesale enslavement of women, and relocate to the Jabari-Lands to bring the guilty husbands and fathers to justice. Soon they are leaders of a fast-growing movement fighting for the rights of all people to live free of torture, privation, or neglect.

Black Panther (Vol. 6) #2 (Jul. 2016)
The Midnight Angels find greater purpose saving people who need them, rather than defending a king who does not.

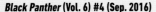

BURNING NATION

As Wakanda descends into civil war, the People, together with their secret allies Ezekiel Stane, Vanisher, and Fenris, seek alliance with rapidly expanding third force the Midnight Angels. However, the recently liberated women of this new faction have no intention of trading old masters for new ones masquerading as friends and equals. T'Challa, meanwhile, turns Tetu's technology against him, and goes hunting with his own imported team, the Crew!

"We are Wakanda. We will not be terrorized. We are terror itself."

T'CHALLA

Black Panther (Vol. 6) #8 (Jan. 2017)
Defying the laws of physics and magic, T'Challa and Manifold seek Shuri's soul in the realms beyond.

Black Panther (Vol. 6) #1 (Jun. 2016) *The People's first strike is to manipulate T'Challa's bodyguards into firing on peacefully protesting Vibranium miners.*

SHURI'S FATE

Long believed dead, Queen Shuri's spirit resides in the Djalia. In this plane of collective Wakandan memory, the former Black Panther is granted great power and instructed in her people's history by a ghostly griot—an African loremaster—disguised as her mother, Ramonda. As Wakandan strife intensifies, T'Challa performs a scientific miracle and brings his sister back for the final battle.

POWER POLITICS

The cataclysmic clash between all factions sees Shuri lead the living, and her brother T'Challa, as King of the Dead, command deceased Black Panthers in an epic struggle that saves Wakanda from tyranny. Shuri and T'Challa then seek to avoid future conflict by turning to ancient wisdom and understanding the needs of their people. Their solution is to embrace democracy and create a constitutional monarchy.

Black Panther (Vol. 6) #11 (Apr. 2017) *The living and the dead unite to defend Wakanda when the People launch their invasion.*

181

A NATION UNDER ATTACK

Reluctantly reclaiming his throne, T'Challa is faced with rebuilding his thrice-shattered land and reuniting a disillusioned and fragmented populace. With Wakanda at its lowest ebb, revolutionaries, opportunists, and outright villains all see a chance to strike a decisive blow for change or personal gain.

"Never leave an enemy behind."

TETU

TETU

Former student of reformer Changamire, Tetu hates monarchy and seeks a different way: one that will leave him as steward of the nation. Many recent disasters have resulted in a loss of wealth and status for Wakandans, allowing Tetu and fellow subversive Zenzi to exploit general dissatisfaction with these turn of events. As the People, Tetu and Zenzi begin a merciless campaign of terror and sedition. Crucial to the campaign's success are Tetu's nature-twisting magical abilities and the emotion-warping power of co-conspirator Zenzi.

ZENZI

As a Nigandan child, Zenzi suffers the prejudice of privileged, arrogant Wakandans. When her homeland is invaded by Killmonger, she is held in a detention camp, but escapes by using newfound emotion-manipulating abilities. Fleeing to Wakanda, Zenzi meets Tetu and, as terrorist cell the People, they use foreign money, Nigandan soldiers, and radical rhetoric to force regime change. The People conspire to overthrow the monarchy using Zenzi's powers, magnifying unrest, and transforming their followers into adrenaline-mutated monsters.

EZEKIEL STANE

Outlaw industrialist and economic opportunist Zeke Stane trades nanite surveillance technology and advanced repulsor weaponry for Tetu's promise to grant him his own Wakandan province. The devices are used to turn ordinary dissidents into unwitting spies and powerful suicide bombers. When the People are defeated, Stane and his superhuman flunkies— the Vanisher, the Fenris twins, and Doctor Faustus—switch to "Plan B," in which they attempt to seize Wakanda for themselves.

MIDNIGHT ANGELS

Rebel *Dora Milaje* Aneka and Ayo flee the Royal Bodyguard corps and become protectors of thousands of women and children abused and enslaved by rural Wakandan sub-chiefs. Their "No One Man" movement rejects T'Challa's authority and they initially ally themselves with the People. On realizing Tetu and his followers are worse than the tribal chiefs they oppose, the Midnight Angels switch sides. They become part of Black Panther's new democratic, constitutional government.

DOCTOR FAUSTUS

Corrupt Austrian psychologist Dr. Johann Fennhoff, a.k.a. Doctor Faustus, uses manipulation and mind-control to convince his patients to commit suicide. Moving to the U.S., Faustus' murderous scientific curiosity and sheer greed bring him up against Captain America and Spider-Man. After working with the Red Skull and far-right organizations such as the National Force, Faustus is hired by Zeke Stane to destroy T'Challa and his allies through psychological means.

CURING GALACTUS

The Ultimates' mission to make the universe a safer place begins by removing the most imminent threat to life: world-consuming Galactus. However, eliminating or imprisoning an omnipotent force of cosmic destruction is not efficient. The team have a better solution in mind...

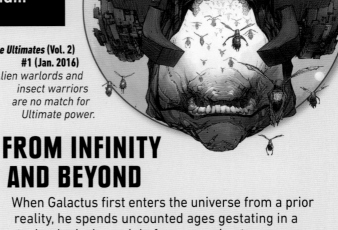

The Ultimates (Vol. 2) #1 (Jan. 2016) Alien warlords and insect warriors are no match for Ultimate power.

SETTING UP SHOP

To speed up solving universal problems, T'Challa allocates vast scientific and financial resources to the Triskelion Building in Manhattan. One wing becomes the new Wakandan Embassy while the second houses the international Alpha Flight Program. The third contains facilities and technicians dedicated to servicing the Ultimates—Earth's most sophisticated science heroes, tasked with averting cosmic catastrophes. The team's first assignment begins as Adam Brashear and Captain Marvel zero in on their prime target—Galactus...

The Ultimates (Vol. 2) #1 (Jan. 2016) The arrival of Galactus' solar-system dwarfing worldship signals the imminent end of another alien civilization, unless the Ultimates' risky scheme succeeds.

FROM INFINITY AND BEYOND

When Galactus first enters the universe from a prior reality, he spends uncounted ages gestating in a technological womb before emerging to consume planets. The Ultimates track down the Devourer's primal incubator and find it being used to mind-control an entire world. By confiscating it, Spectrum and Ms. America become planetary liberators.

TALKING TO A GOD

The Ultimates invade Galactus' worldship *Taa II*, where the space god is preparing for another battle with humankind. Instead, these lowly mortal trespassers attempt to negotiate with the all-powerful death-dealer. Sadly, reason proves ineffective against the Devourer's constant hunger. As T'Challa suspected, force would be required to resolve the matter.

The Ultimates (Vol. 2) #2 (Feb. 2016) The toughest part of the Ultimates' scheme is getting Galactus to notice them.

The Ultimates (Vol. 2) #2 (Feb. 2016) T'Challa's deft Kimoyo reprogramming rapidly evolves Galactus into the benign creature the Universe intended him to be.

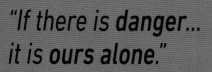

The Ultimates (Vol. 2) #1 (Jan. 2016) Black Panther, Spectrum, Blue Marvel, America Chavez, and Captain Marvel unite in a devious scheme to make an ally of the ultimate enemy.

GRAVE TO CRADLE

The star-god is caught off-guard when the Ultimates produce his ancient incubator and force him into it. T'Challa links the chamber to his Kimoyo supercomputer operating system and reprograms the incubator to overfeed Galactus with energy until he has more than he will ever need to sustain his existence.

LIFEBRINGER

The plan succeeds. Galactus emerges from the incubator replete with power. Without a word of gratitude, the transformed Devourer heads back into the cosmos and begins reviving the innumerable worlds he had previously consumed and left as dead husks. His new astral mission is to seed these planets with the potential to sustain new life.

The Ultimates (Vol. 2) #2 (Feb. 2016) Free of his all-consuming hunger, Galactus starts resurrecting long-dead worlds.

THE ULTIMATES

All too aware that the universe is perilously fragile, Black Panther and Captain Marvel gather a mighty team of troubleshooters to anticipate cosmic threats, assess potential solutions, and deal with them preemptively and permanently.

BLUE MARVEL

In the 1960s, physicist Adam Brashear is accidentally mutated by Negative Zone radiation and develops a vast range of antimatter-fueled powers. He becomes the masked hero Blue Marvel. However, when his ethnicity as a black man is exposed, the U.S. president orders him to retire to ease flaring racial tensions. From that point on, Brashear uses his gifts covertly and infrequently to prevent social unrest. Following decades of self-imposed exile, Brashear emerges from the shadows to battle his oldest enemy and joins Luke Cage's Mighty Avengers in defending New York from Thanos. Brilliant and immensely powerful, Blue Marvel is the moral backbone of T'Challa's problem-solving squad.

CAPTAIN MARVEL

Military intelligence officer Carol Danvers is transformed into a multi-powered superhuman after being caught in an explosion from a Kree device. She operates as a hero under a number of different codenames. Working with the Starjammers, X-Men, and Avengers, she saves Earth and many other worlds, eventually taking the name Captain Marvel in honor of the Kree warrior, Mar-Vell, who first inspired her. Carol devises the concept of the Ultimates, strategizing with Black Panther to create the perfect team to head off cosmic-level threats. Her hard-line views on preemptive intervention bring her into conflict with Tony Stark, sparking a second civil war among Earth's Super Heroes.

SPECTRUM

Able to manipulate light after surviving bombardment by extradimensional energies, Monica Rambeau becomes Spectrum. Monica trains with and then leads the Avengers and covert super-squad Nextwave. She forms a close working relationship with T'Challa, helping him against Killmonger in Niganda, and in eradicating a vampire invasion of New Orleans alongside a specialist team including Doctor Voodoo, Luke Cage, and Blade. Her immense power-set, strategic brilliance, and commanding presence on the battlefield make her an invaluable resource to the Ultimates as they confront situations far beyond the scope of ordinary mortals.

MS. AMERICA

Unique throughout all reality, teenager America Chavez leaves her magical home in the Utopian Parallel. She begins righting injustices throughout the multiverse using her ability to travel between universes. After saving the world and several parallel realities with the Teen Brigade and Young Avengers, the hard-headed hero initially feels that she works better on her own until she is recruited for the Ultimates. Driven to protect the helpless, she pushes herself relentlessly and clashes with Captain Marvel over the policy of preventative policing during the second superhuman civil war. The dispute leads to the Ultimates breaking up, until they are reunited by Anti-Man at the command of Galactus the Lifebringer.

ANTI-MAN

Conner Sims gains antimatter powers in the same accident that creates Blue Marvel. Transformed into sentient energy, Sims is slowly driven mad and resolves to expunge humanity after his brother dies in a clash between the Ku Klux Klan and the F.B.I. His battles with Brashear expose Blue Marvel's identity, and force the hero into politically-expedient exile. Dormant for decades, Anti-Man returns to attack the Mighty Avengers, bringing Brashear out of retirement to remove Anti-Man from the multiverse. Banished to the Exo-Space beyond creation, Sims is rescued and reformed by the Ultimates. He becomes an ally, and as herald of Galactus the Lifebringer, Anti-Man reunites the team following the second superhuman civil war.

The Ultimates (Vol. 2) #5 (May 2016)
As T'Challa's cosmic troubleshooters, the Ultimates, investigate time-travel's damaging impact on reality, they discover Eternity—the embodiment of all creation—in shackles. Freeing the cosmic being turns out to be the Ultimates' most fraught and critical mission.

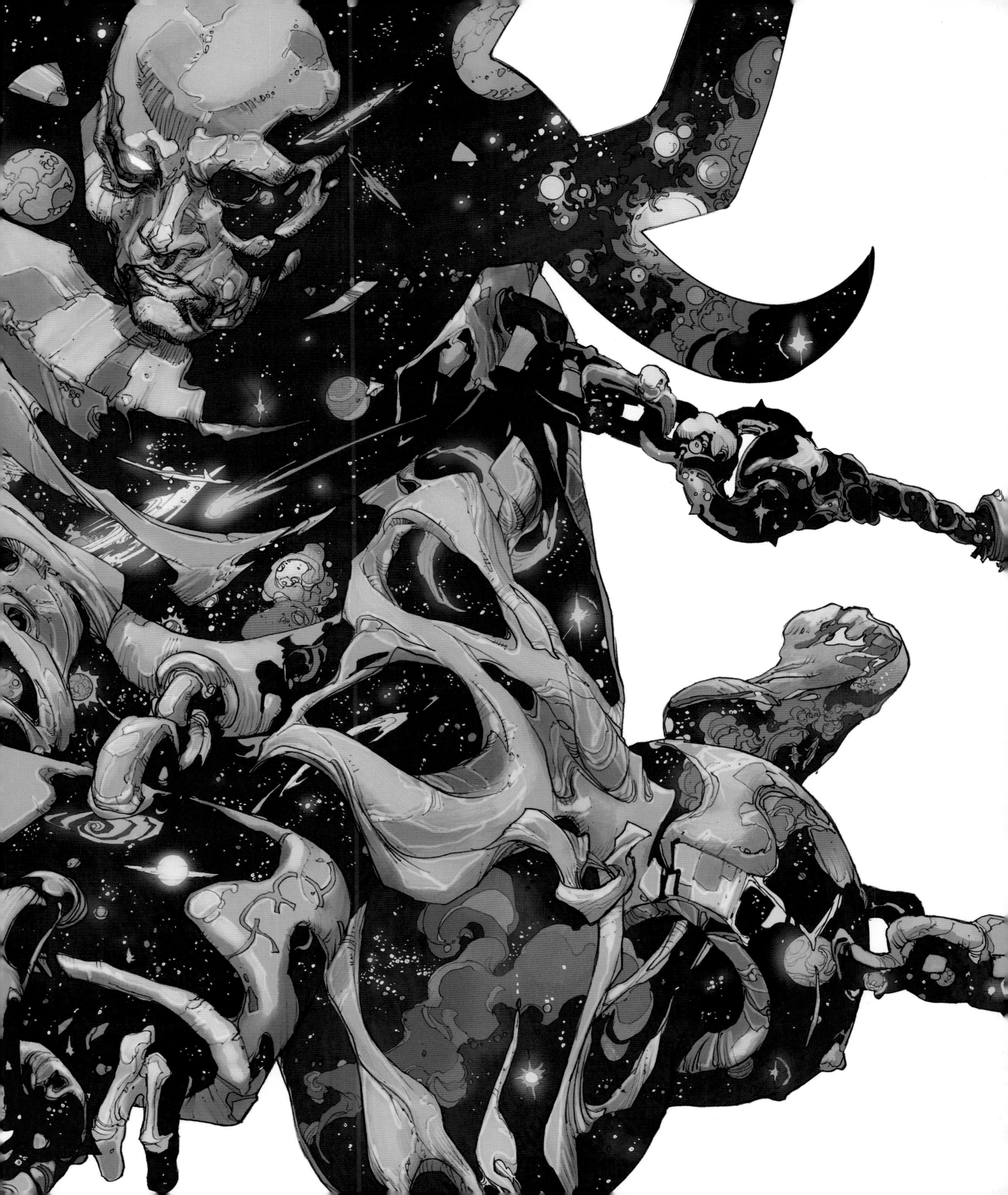

THE CREW

With Wakanda torn apart by civil war against terrorist cell the People, and a growing mutiny within the *Dora Milaje*, T'Challa forms a team of loyal, battle-hardened warriors to help his cause.

MISTY KNIGHT

Street-smart cop Mercedes "Misty" Knight loses her arm in a bombing incident. Pensioned off, she is given a bionic limb built by Tony Stark and sets up as a private detective. An undercover specialist, she increasingly becomes involved with Super Heroes such as Iron Fist—with whom she has a romantic relationship—and his long-time ally, Luke Cage. Using her street contacts and superhuman connections, Misty forms and leads a number of teams, such as the Daughters of the Dragon, Heroes for Hire, and Misty Knight's Crew.

At Luke Cage's request, Misty joins T'Challa's counterinsurgency unit the Crew and is crucial in extending the team's remit to tackle crises in the U.S.

LUKE CAGE

Although an incredibly powerful and capable individual, Cage often enjoys working as part of a team. Growing up on the streets and having been an innocent victim of state-sanctioned injustice, he well knows the difference between "legal" and "righteous."

When his friend T'Challa asks for his aid in an undercover mission that goes beyond the bounds of usual Super Hero exploits, Cage gathers together trusted allies of a similar disposition. These heroes help the Black Panther root out the real forces stirring up dangerous rebellion in Wakanda. They become the Crew, a remorseless team ready to uncover and deal with the hidden sponsors of the deadly terrorist cell known as the People.

*"If you want to save a kingdom...call in **the Crew**."*

LUKE CAGE

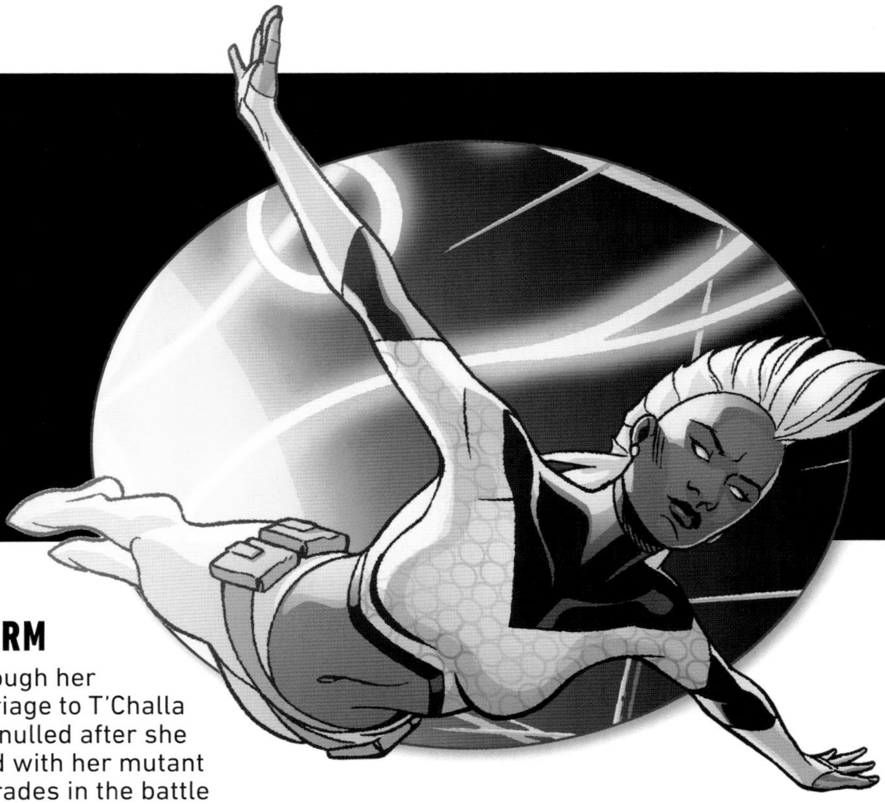

STORM

Although her marriage to T'Challa is annulled after she sided with her mutant comrades in the battle between the Avengers and the X-Men, Ororo's love for him remains undiminished, as does her devotion to the people of Wakanda. When the People commence their terrorist outrages in Wakanda, she immediately offers her help and becomes a key player in the Black Panther's counterattack strategies.

After the conflict's conclusion, Ororo remains close to T'Challa and her new band of brothers and sisters, reuniting the Crew when their services are needed to confront evil and injustice.

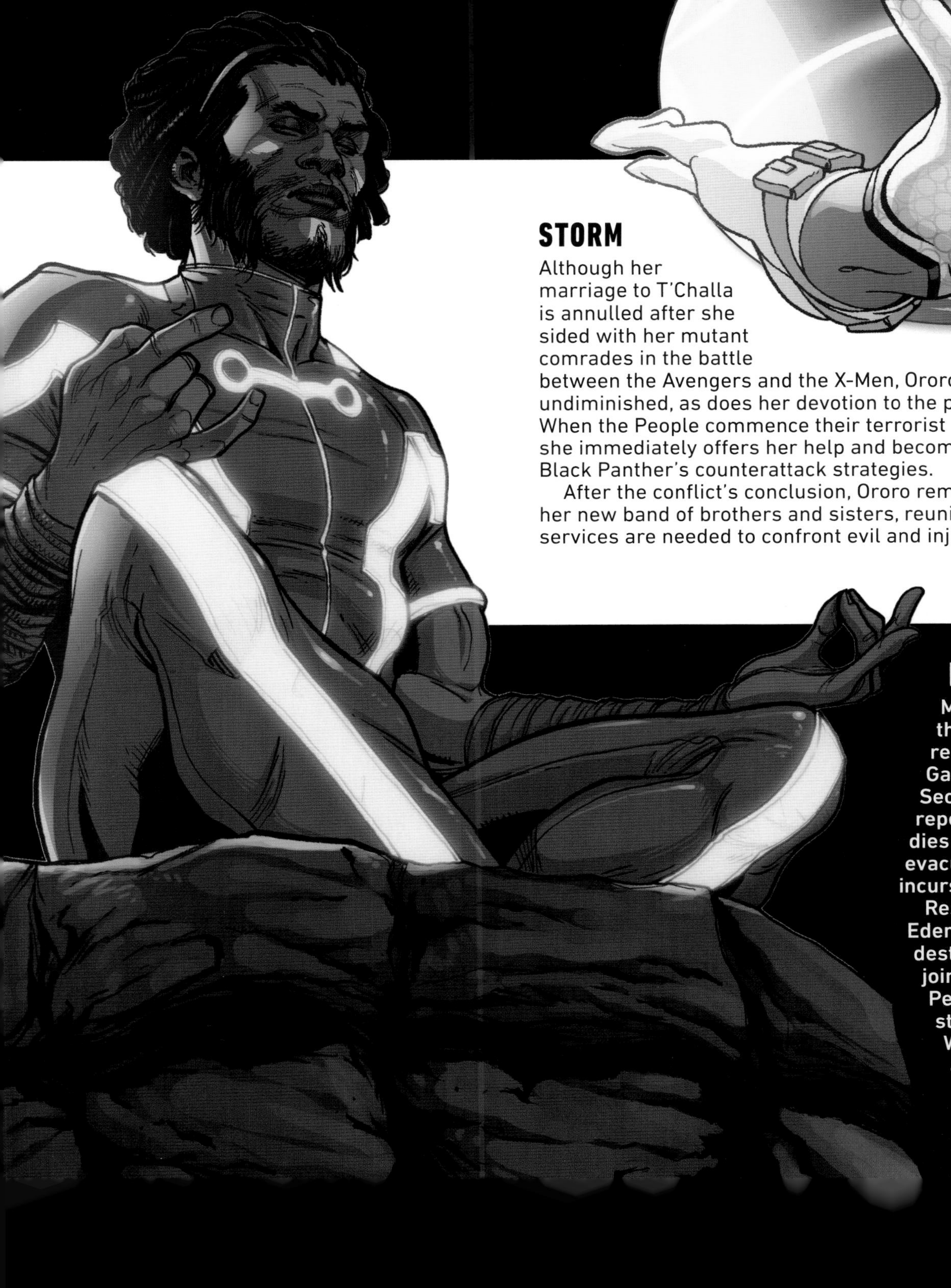

MANIFOLD

Mutant Eden Fesi is trained in the use of his teleportation and reality-molding by X-Men ally Gateway. As one of Nick Fury's Secret Avengers, Manifold has repeatedly saved the world, and dies transporting the Illuminati's evacuation team to safety during the incursion of collapsing universes.

Resurrected when reality is reborn, Eden has no memory of his or Earth's destruction and rebirth, and eagerly joins T'Challa's fight against the People. As well as transporting strike teams of *Hatut Zeraze*—Wakanda's elite squad of assassins—to combat zones, Eden is the backbone of T'Challa's Crew. His power even calls Shuri back from the spiritual plane of the Djalia to the physical world

THE LANDS BEYOND

Although rooted in the sciences of the physical world, Wakanda is also inextricably linked to many metaphysical planes where higher beings dwell. Extraordinary and accessible, these spiritual domains exert constant demands on the Wakandan people, shaping their lives on a daily basis.

DEATH'S DOMAIN

Death is inevitable, but the passage linking the living to the afterlife is a corridor where the recently deceased can bargain with—or battle against—the skeletal embodiment of their fate. When T'Challa is ambushed by Doctor Doom and seemingly dies, witchman Zawavari sends Queen Ororo into this twilight realm to sacrifice her life for her husband's.

Black Panther (Vol. 5) #2 (May 2009)

BAST'S REALM

The Panther Spirit has male and female forms and both reside in a constantly shifting realm that responds to the state-of-mind of its visitors. Bast uses this lair to confer with her current earthly avatar and judge supplicants attempting to assume the role and duties of the Black Panther.

Black Panther (Vol. 3) #21 (Aug. 2000)

NECROPOLIS

Situated near Lake Nyanza, Necropolis is a city of tombs and mausoleums outside Wakanda's capital Birnin Zana. For thousands of years, it has stored the bodies of fallen Black Panthers. It is also a nexus adjoining Bast's realm, where deceased ancestral Panthers can cross back to the physical plane to confer with, advise, or even admonish the latest in their warrior line.

Fantastic Four (Vol. 1) #608 (Sep. 2012)

DJALIA

Wakandans can trace their proud achievements back for millennia through the unbroken line of the Panther Cult. However, some gifted individuals are capable of much more. Griots are wandering poets who safeguard the oral history of African nations, and many Wakandan tribes can actually relive their people's development by entering the Djalia, a higher spiritual plane of collective ancestral memory.

This otherworldly realm incorporates all the experiences and knowledge of every Wakandan who ever lived—intimately linking searchers to their past through Griot spirit guides. When Queen Shuri enters the Djalia, a Griot taking the guise of her mother Ramonda, helps Shuri understand her extraordinary new powers and even prepare for resurrection after death.

Black Panther (Vol. 6) #2 (Jul. 2016)

ACROSS THE MULTIVERSE

The multiverse contains an infinite number of universes, each with a designated number. Most universes have a planet Earth, the best known being Earth-616. These worlds seem remarkably similar, until you take a closer look. A multitude of Black Panthers exists across all realities, and though they appear alike, their differences are as great as their similarities.

EARTH-8441

When war between the U.S. and Wakanda threatens the safety of Earth, President Luke Cage averts disaster. He gives his daughter, Danielle, in marriage to T'Wari, the son of King T'Challa and Queen Storm. The officiating priestess is reigning Black Panther, Shuri.

EARTH-9997

After Inhuman monarch Black Bolt releases Terrigen Mists globally, all of humanity mutates and gains super-powers. King T'Challa of Wakanda transforms into a human/panther cross, in accord with the spirits of the great beasts of Earth.

EARTH-982

T'Chaka II (a.k.a. Coal Tiger) is the son of Wakandan king and former Avenger, T'Challa. He is an official diplomat, but occasionally moonlights as a hero with the superteam A-Next. He uses his supernatural ability to transform himself into a powerful "were-panther."

EARTH-1119

On Earth-1119, T'Challa and Storm's son, T'Chaka II, is ambushed and presumed killed by the sound-manipulating villain Klaw, soon after the youth has won his birthright. Instead, the exuberant hero has been plucked from his homeworld to battle multiversal anomalies as Panther, part of a trans-dimensional superteam called the Exiles.

EARTH-355

Super Hero Coal Tiger is the sole survivor of his doomed world when he is recruited by the dimension-hopping Gatherers for their war against the Avengers. Coal Tiger chooses to die of an agonizing temporal imbalance, rather than cure himself by killing and replacing his Earth-616 counterpart.

EARTH-2301

King and chief shaman of Wakanda, T'Challa can summon guardian spirits to inhabit and transform his body. Although his favored form is the feral Black Panther, he can also become the high-flying Falcon, whose powers are vital to combat his sister, Doctor Doom.

EARTH-2992

In a dystopian alternate future, in the year 2099, the world is ruthlessly ruled by Doctor Doom. A powerless rebel named K'Shamba leads Wakanda's underground resistance. However, none of this Black Panther's comrades realizes their leader is actually Doom's secret lackey.

EARTH-1610

On a harsh world of Ultimate heroes and villains, mutant T'Challa Udaku fails the Trial of the Panther ritual and is seriously injured. So King T'Chaka gives his maimed son to the American Weapon X program, where he is rebuilt with the same modifications as Wolverine. He goes on to become an agent of S.H.I.E.L.D.

INDEX

Page numbers in **bold** refer to main entries.

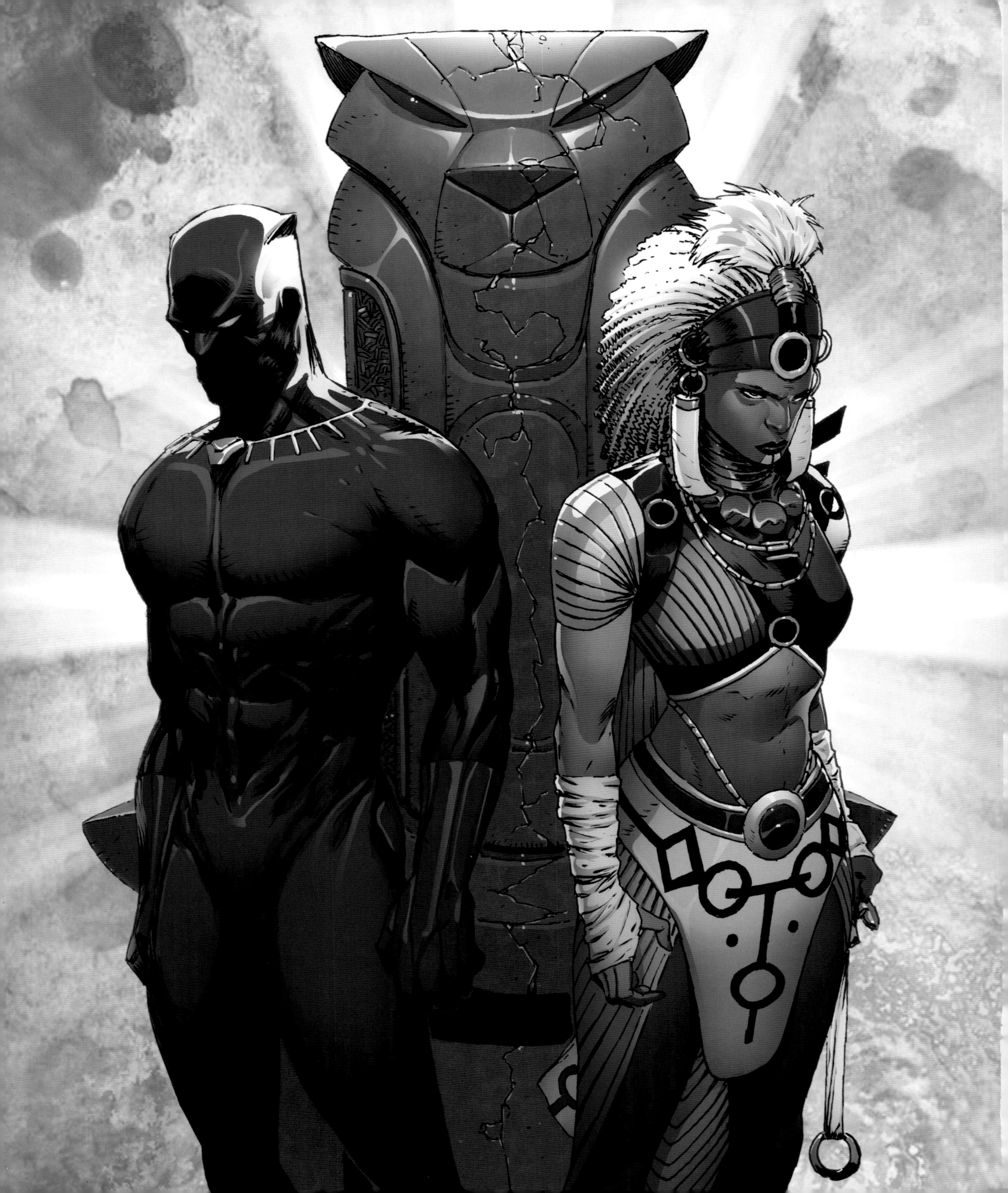